Heroes and Villains in Welsh History

Heroes and Villains in Welsh History

A New History of Wales

Edited by

H. V. Bowen

Gomer

Published in 2012 by
Gomer Press, Llandysul, Ceredigion, SA44 4JL

ISBN 978 1 84851 485 0

This book is published with the financial support of the
Welsh Books Council.

Printed and bound in Wales at
Gomer Press, Llandysul, Ceredigion

Acknowledgements

The essays reprinted in this book first appeared in the *Western Mail* newspaper in March and April 2011. They followed on from a highly successful first series of essays, which was then published by Gomer as a book in 2011: *A New History of Wales: Myths and Realities in Welsh History.* The partnership between the *Western Mail* and History Research Wales remains a unique one, not just in the United Kingdom but in world terms. Nowhere else are academic historians given so many column inches to write whatever they want about their chosen theme, which in this case was heroes and villains in Welsh history. For making this happen I thank Alan Edmunds, Editor of the *Western Mail*, and Ceri Gould-Thomas, Executive Editor, Media Wales. I also thank Tony Woolway, Chief Librarian of Media Wales, for his help with the selection of many of the images that appear in the book; and Ceri Wyn Jones of Gomer Press who saw the book through to publication despite some very tight deadlines. The essays are published more or less as they first appeared in the newspaper although, in addition to basic re-formatting, some small alterations and corrections have been made. The essays have been slightly re-ordered, and they are prefaced by an introductory essay written by Peter Stead, which first appeared in the *Western Mail's* Saturday Magazine.

H. V. Bowen, Swansea, Easter Monday 2012

Picture Acknowledgements

The contributors and publishers gratefully acknowledge the following sources of images: Western Mail/Media Wales: 13, 21, 22, 32, 66, 76, 77, 80, 84, 85, 87, 96, 99, 105, 106, 112, 115, 128, 131, 134, 137, 141, 143, 149, 153, 154, 162, 163, 164, 166, 169, 173, 174, 176, 178, 179, 181, 183, 184, 187, 188, 189; Anthony Griffiths: 14, 26; Thomas Halliwell: 18 (top); Madeleine Gray: 18 (bottom), 19; Hugh Olliff: 27, 53, 65; Ken Day: 35; Helen J. Nicholson: 38, 40, 41, 42, 43; Jeremy Moore: 32 (top), 46, 79 [from *Wales at Water's Edge*, Gomer, 2012]; the Trustees of Manorbier Castle and Monddi Diamond Press: 49; Paul White: 55, 88, 107 [all from *Ancestral Houses: the Lost Mansions of Wales*, Gomer 2012]; National Museums and Galleries of Wales: 59, 73; David Pearl: 63; Richard Pawelko: 74, 108; Huw Evans Sports Agency: 92, 135, 196, 197, 198; National Library of Wales: 93; Richard Stanton: 100; Gethin Matthews: 122, 123, 125; Sian Rhiannon Williams: 145, 147; BBC: 160, 171; Colorsport: 193.

It has not been possible to trace the owner of copyright in every case. The publishers apologise for any omission and will be pleased to remedy any oversight when reprinting.

Contents

Contents (*continued*)

Introduction

Peter Stead

To a far greater extent than we admit, heroes and villains play a crucial role in shaping each of our own individual identities as well as the pattern of our social and political lives. This tends to be the case in societies that feel it important to consolidate a sense of national identity. From the days of our earliest childhood, parents, teachers and the media are both consciously and unconsciously furnishing our minds with a pantheon of heroes and an attendant rogues' gallery.

Undoubtedly there is both a personal and national need for heroes but the role assigned to the selected 'legends' (to use the term now beloved by the media) is often a difficult one to sustain. Both heroes and villains tend to be rooted in mythology rather than objective and factual analysis. Of course, the job of historians is to demythologise the past but, nevertheless, historians have an exciting story to tell and out of its complexity authentic heroes and villains emerge.

During the Millennium celebrations I was asked to comment on an HTV poll in which viewers had been asked to select their Welsh Personality of the Millennium. The clear winner with 40% of the vote was the politician Aneurin Bevan. The vast majority of HTV's viewers lived in urban South Wales and, at a time of growing crisis in the NHS, it is not difficult to see why the once MP for Ebbw Vale should be the stand-out hero in a thousand years of Welsh history. In any analysis of Bevan's career, however, we should recall the comments of the Welsh Tory MP, originally from Neath, who told me that it was Bevan's bitter jibe that the 'Tories were lower than vermin' that had led to his own entry into politics. We should also consider the comments of the Welsh miners' leader who explained that many communists 'did not completely trust' Bevan and regarded him as 'unreliable and erratic'. The miners' leaders were not alone in speaking of the two Bevans: the one seen in Soho restaurants with his mates, and the one who visited his Ebbw Vale constituency.

Even in Wales there was always a whispering campaign against Bevan. Prophets, after all, are not to be honoured in their own country. And, of course, one person's hero is another person's villain. It is certainly the case that the identification of any hero will soon be followed by a debunking. Perhaps Sebastian Faulks is right to argue that heroes only belong in literary epics, and villains in the theatre and pantomime. Ideally all mythologies and pantheons need to be critically and scholarly analysed. The true heroes (and villains) will emerge all the more clearly defined when the sheer complexity of their careers and decision-making is established.

What has delighted me about this selection of heroes my colleagues have chosen is the emphasis on what we call 'ordinary men and women'. The actual ordeal of living through history was rarely easy and neither has it been easy for historians to bring alive and pay tribute to those men and women who endured hardship, privation, physical labour and warfare, and who yet created a society in which family values, ethical values, community spirit and cultural fulfilment were fundamental. When we think back on our history, it is difficult to deny that it has been working men and women that have been the real heroes. The historian E.P. Thompson charged his colleagues with the task of 'rescuing these true heroes from anonymity'.

All those men and women needed to be sustained by their own heroes. Politicians and union leaders were often set up as heroes but feet of clay were all too frequently identified as betrayals occurred. True sainthood was rarely bestowed: there was the martyr Dic Penderyn, the founding father Keir Hardie, and, in the Rhondda, the miners' leader John Hopla. Imprisoned during the Tonypandy Riots and subsequently prominent in the Fed, Hopla is commemorated outside the Llwynypia Institute, of which he was president, with a plaque that says 'Thy Work Till Death Hath Made Thy Life Immortal'. Every person active in public life should be subject to what I call 'the Hopla test'.

In my own family there was also need for religious heroes drawn either from history or our own times. In the Wales of the first half of the last century, all the religious denominations had their star preachers, charismatic figures known for their oratory and their ability to generate a *hwyl* to which the deacons in the *sedd fawr* would respond noisily. These men were admired as much as the Hollywood movie stars many of them resembled. My father and my uncles would travel miles to hear these heroes. In contrast, my mother, a devout Christian, had grown up the daughter of a chapel secretary, and having spent so many Sundays feeding ministers at her home, she retained a suspicion of them. She saw them as 'scroungers, out for themselves and their children'.

Nevertheless I find it surprising that, even in these secular times, historians do not make more of religious heroes. We know little about St David apart from the earth lifting him up, but we cherish him because he confirms our sense of our being Celtic Christians and because he has given us our most reassuring and popular Christian name. At school, our houses were named after Celtic saints: Dyfan, Illtyd, Cadoc and, my favourite, the one to which I was assigned, Baruc. More real to us were the martyrs of the Reformation, the translators of The Bible and the great hymn writers like Pantycelyn and Ann Griffiths. The greatest inspiration of all came from the life of Mary Jones who in 1800 had walked thirty miles to Bala to buy a Bible.

I am glad that teachers have been identified as heroes. Teachers played a fundamentally important part in creating modern Wales. Authors such as Emlyn Williams and Alun Richards have placed the pupil/teacher relationship at the centre of our culture, and the biographical writing on Richard Burton, Stanley Baker, Sian Phillips, Gareth Edwards and almost all the stars of our popular culture highlights the crucial role of individual teachers. It was women teachers, the first professional women in Wales, who gave the country its backbone in the early twentieth century. But we can all name that Miss X with whom we first fell in love, the brilliant teacher who first identified the particular talent that was our own, and the utter professionalism of the teachers who prepared us for the big examinations. Just as vividly, we remember the sense of community as we joked about our teachers, glorying in their nicknames and, of course, developing the Gothic horror of the hated villains on the staff, the sadists who caned us and rapped rulers on our knuckles as they condemned us once more to impositions and detention. One way or another they made us into the men and women we are.

In the Wales of today it is absolutely vital that within the general title of Heroes and Villains we look at industrialists and entrepreneurs. We pride ourselves on our love of history and we openly acknowledge that both our personal and national identities are rooted in history. We are less keen to accept the fact that history is a battleground in which British Imperialists, Welsh Nationalists and Social Democratic and Marxist historians have between them set the agenda. In the process the most important event in Welsh history, the Industrial Revolution of the 18th and 19th centuries, tends to be misunderstood. Imagine how different the Wales of today would be if our popular histories had been written exclusively by economic historians talking of industry as 'the only hope of the poor', of the importance of economic growth and productivity, and urging us to become entrepreneurs rather than teachers, broadcasters and actors.

In my childhood there was much talk of preachers, teachers, and movie stars but hardly any mention of business or industry. I remember once sitting with my steelworker uncle above a field above Merthyr: he pointed to the field and said 'that was once ours but the Marquis of Bute took it from us'. It was years before I discovered who the Butes were. A teacher then argued that the Marquis's decision to build Cardiff Docks was probably the biggest financial undertaking by one man in history. His story should be central to our study of history. Years later that same uncle was reading about vital developments at the Steel Company of Wales, Port Talbot, and he came across the name of its boss, Sir Frederick Cartwright. 'Cartwright is a genius', he said, 'I worked under him in the Dowlais works: he really knows about steel.' Of course in Wales we need to study and understand the riots and strikes that the Marxists highlight but we could all have done with spending more time talking about the genius (and if need be the villainy) of our industrial, technological and scientific geniuses.

Historians must always start with the telling of the story. Our penchant for myths and legends has tended to blind us to the sheer thrill of narrative. The story of our small mountainous country is well worth the telling, but for the early centuries we have to get past the writings of the poets and romancers who invented and sustained the notion of Wales and, in so doing, relied heavily on heroes. In this they were more effective than any modern spin doctors.

We will never know whether our great princes were particularly charming or had a sense of humour, but we are able to comment on their military prowess, whether they slaughtered their defeated enemies and the degree to which they were respected intellectually. We can assume that they would be in favour of Devolution but, in most respects, they come to us from a past that is 'a different country'. In that Millennium poll Owain Glyndŵr, with 19% of the votes, came second to Bevan. We know little about Glyndŵr as a man but what is crucial is that his story is exciting and that gave the romancers, not least Shakespeare, every basis for creating a real national hero.

Astonishingly and disgracefully, David Lloyd George, undoubtedly the greatest Welshman of modern times, came seventh in the poll with only 5% of the vote. Undoubtedly his opposition to trade union militants and his visit to Hitler reduced his standing. However the real problem was the manner in which we allowed his name and reputation to become a music-hall joke. We might not have read the absolutely gripping story of British Cabinet politics between 1905 and 1922, but we all joked that 'Lloyd George knew' or possibly 'was', 'my father'. Meanwhile British historians had secured the Churchill myth. In fact Winston himself had always acknowledged that LG was the master. We have let down one of our greatest heroes. Just think how the USA would have treated his memory if he had been their president.

In the HTV poll Gareth Edwards (8%) was fourth and Richard Burton (5%)

was sixth. This was evidence enough of the extent to which our nation is dominated by popular culture (John Charles was strangely absent). Gareth reigns supreme as the greatest rugby player ever (whispers about his never having been much of a club player were suppressed). Burton continues to fascinate us although there are few people left alive who saw him on stage, and in only a handful of his movies did he deploy his full powers. He remains a hero partly because he consciously embodied all the qualities that the people of Wales admired. He looked good, he spoke English beautifully and, wherever he went in the world, he told his admirers that he was Welsh. He often added that, on the whole, he would have been happier if he had been a coal miner who had published a book and played rugby for Wales.

But there was something else. In his most convincing roles Burton played kings, princes, generals or priests and in so doing exuded a natural authority and confidence. In that respect, for all his weaknesses, he remains the president or king that we have never had. He gave us an indication of what true Welsh leadership could amount to.

Peter Stead with the statue of another Welsh hero and villain, Dylan Thomas

The river Usk, where Cadoc's
parents bathed in midwinter

1

WINIFRED AND CADOC: SAINTS OR SINNERS?

Madeleine Gray

We all think we know what a saint is like. Mother Teresa, Padre Pio, Francis of Assisi – they share the lives of the poor, they care for the sick, they feed the hungry, they sacrifice their lives for others. The early medieval period in Wales is sometimes called the 'Age of Saints' because of the holy men and women who led the church, but they were saints of a very different kind. Like the stories of Arthur and the Mabinogi, their lives have been rewritten many times, to suit changing values and changing circumstances. They were figures of power, like the heroes of legend – and to modern eyes some of them can even seem more like villains.

SAINT CADOC – MIRACLES, MARRIAGE AND MONKS

Cadoc was one of the most important of these saints in South Wales. Born into the royal families of Gwynllwg and Brycheiniog, he worked miracles even before his birth. Strange lights shone in his parents' house and the cellars were miraculously filled with food. An angel announced his birth and summoned the hermit Meuthi to baptise and teach him. A holy well sprang up for his baptism and afterwards flowed with wine and milk. He grew up to be a great leader: churches all over South Wales were dedicated to him, and he founded the great monastery of Llancarfan, near Barry in the Vale of Glamorgan. (The lovely medieval church at Llancarfan is probably on the site of his monastery. It has a very large oval churchyard, which is usually a sign of an old site. The wall paintings which have recently been discovered there, though, are much later in date.)

There is a darker side to the story, though. Cadoc had a disastrous impact on many of those close to him. He destroyed his parents' marriage, persuading them to take vows of celibacy. According to the story, they tried to remain together, bathing in the Usk in midwinter to quell their desires, but eventually they were forced to move apart. Cadoc's father, Gwynllyw, founded the monastery at Newport which bore his name (now St Woollos) and his mother, Gwladus, left for the hills above Gelli-gaer where she also founded a religious community. A sad end for a marriage that began with the young couple, wildly in love, eloping from her father's court at Brecon and escaping over the mountains.

Even Cadoc's monastery was not without its problems. Having got the community established, he went off to Ireland to study and teach. When he returned three years later, he found the monastery in ruins. Furious, he forced the monks back to manual labour, dragging timber from the woods to begin the work of reconstruction. Two stags came out of the forest to help them, which is said to be why the stream running past the monastery is called Nant Carfan, the Stag Brook.

But Cadoc was a persuasive and charismatic figure, and attracted devoted followers and students. One Lent he took two of his disciples from Llancarfan on a retreat to Flat Holm and then on to what is now Barry Island. When they reached Barry, the students realised they had left Cadoc's prayer book behind. He sent them back to get it, in a storm, then watched from the headland as their little ship foundered and they were drowned. But the book was brought miraculously to shore. This might make him a hero to librarians, but if he was an academic nowadays he would be told to think more carefully about student retention.

In many of the stories about Cadoc, he is vengeful and unforgiving in the extreme. He blinded King Rhun of Gwynedd, who had tried to burn one of Cadoc's barns. At his command the earth opened and swallowed Sawyl Benuchel, who had plundered the monastery at Llancarfan, and some soldiers who had demanded food from him with menaces. Turning the other cheek never seemed to appeal to him.

CADOC AND HIS FELLOW SAINTS AND HEROES

Nor did Cadoc enjoy good relations with the other Welsh saints. St Gildas came to stay with him in Llancarfan, bringing with him a particularly fine bell. Cadoc wanted the bell, Gildas refused to part with it, but the bell then refused to sound until he handed it over. Cadoc even fell out with St David. Behind the story of the great meeting at Llanddewibrefi, when David made the ground rise up so that he could be heard, is a surprisingly modern story of church politics and backstairs manoeuvres. David's lifestyle was so ostentatiously pure that he was suspected of the Pelagian heresy, the idea that you can get into Heaven by your own efforts. David summoned a synod, a church meeting, to sort this out: but he failed to invite Cadoc, possibly because the two men were rivals for the leadership of the church. When Cadoc found out, he was furious. It took a visit from an angel to calm him down.

Statue of St David at Llanddewibrefi

CADOC AND CATTLE

Cadoc even managed to cheat another Welsh hero, King Arthur. A soldier who had killed three of Arthur's knights claimed sanctuary in one of Cadoc's churches. Arthur tried to threaten Cadoc but was afraid to attack him. Eventually they reached a compromise: Cadoc would keep the soldier and give Arthur a herd of cattle as compensation. But when Arthur's followers took the cattle and tried to drive them across the river Usk, the cattle turned into bundles of fern. As with the wizards Math fab Mathonwy and Gwydion in the Mabinogi, Cadoc's power extended over the natural world. Even King Arthur was eventually forced to acknowledge the error of his ways and leave Cadoc in peace.

SAINT WINIFRED, SAINT BEUNO AND THE HOLY WELL

Not all the Welsh saints were as evil-tempered as Cadoc. St Winifred's shrine at Holywell in north-east Wales is still an enormously popular focus for pilgrimage. Winifred is probably best known from the Brother Cadfael novels of Ellis Peters. The first of these, *A Morbid Taste for Bones*, is based around historical events and tells how the monks of Shrewsbury Abbey journeyed to Gwytherin (in the hills south of Colwyn Bay) to acquire Winifred's relics and take them back to Shrewsbury. The prior of Shrewsbury, Robert Pennant, then wrote an account of Winifred's life which depicted her as an innocent girl, killed by a disappointed suitor and brought back to life by her uncle and teacher, St Beuno. After Beuno's death, she looked for another male

Stained-glass window depicting St Winifred

mentor and eventually travelled to Gwytherin, where she entered a nunnery founded by the local saint, Eleri (a man).

But there is also a slightly earlier version of her life, probably written in Wales, in which she is a much more heroic figure. According to this version, Winifred was a strong-minded and independent young woman who chose to devote her life to religion, defying both her father and the local ruler and winning them over. Her father then asked a wandering saint, Beuno, to teach her. They studied together in his remote hermitage without a breath of scandal. She became an acolyte, an assistant priest. She was at home on her own when the rest of the family had gone to church, as she was preparing the necessary items for the mass. The son of the local king was out hunting and came to the house asking for water. Inflamed by her beauty, he begged her first to become his mistress, then to marry him. Winifred first tried to argue with him then outwitted him: she agreed to go with him but asked to be allowed to change into her best clothes, then escaped out of the bedroom window and ran for it.

The young man set spurs to his horse, caught up with her and beheaded her. (Top marks for commitment but not a very good seduction strategy.) But her tutor, Beuno, healed her, and where her head had touched the ground a spring of holy water gushed out. This is the spring which gave its name to Holywell. As far as Beuno was concerned, this was Winifred's miracle, not his, and it meant that Holywell was the place God had given her. He was the one who had to move on. They parted as equals, with mutual blessing, and every year she made him a miraculous cloak which kept out the rain and wind. (As he had gone to live in Snowdonia, this must have been very welcome.)

ROME, RENEWAL AND RELIC

But after a while Winifred wanted to move on. She went to Rome, where she renewed her vows at the shrine of the apostles. There she encountered some new thinking about the religious life. According to the earlier version of her life, it was Winifred who brought St Benedict's new ideas about living in religious communities (as opposed to living as hermits) back to Britain. She summoned a synod, a church gathering of the whole of Britain, which introduced these reforms. Then she retired to Gwytherin, where she founded and led a religious community, and she was eventually buried there. Even after her body was taken to Shrewsbury, the people of Gwytherin claimed to have a relic of her, possibly a book or a bell, housed in an ornately carved wooden chest. A tiny fragment of this reliquary can still be seen in the museum at Holywell but the rest has long gone. Pilgrims to the shrine at Gwytherin carried away pieces of the chest until it virtually disappeared.

The medieval seal of St Asaph

Winifred is shown in medieval stained glass in Llandyrnog in the Vale of Clwyd, as a teacher and religious leader with her vestments and her book. On the medieval seal of the diocese of St Asaph, she is shown holding an abbot's crozier (a symbol of her power). Her fame even spread as far as London. There is a statue of her in the Lady Chapel that Henry VII built at Westminster Abbey. Like the stained glass at Llandyrnog, this shows her as a learned young woman with a book, but in an even more bizarre touch she has her own decapitated head by her side.

CROSS HER AT YOUR PERIL

Like Cadoc, Winifred could be vengeful, but she also protected and cared for her followers. One of the stories about her holy well involves a young servant girl who was being abused by her employers. The girl fled to Winifred's shrine but her mistress continued to beat her even while the girl was clinging to the church door. Eventually Winifred's power was too much for her: the woman's jaw and throat twisted out of shape and stayed like that until she died.

This Winifred of the earlier story is a real hero for the women's movement – tough-minded, fearless, independent, a woman who stood up and said 'No'. The choices she made seem strange to us – rejecting human relationships, living away from the world – but they were her choices. In many ways she reminds us of the women in the stories of the Mabinogi, women like Rhiannon and Elen Lluydawg. Like Rhiannon, Winifred tricked an unwelcome suitor, and like Elen she became a leader and travelled far from her home.

PILGRIMAGE

You can still visit many of the places in the lives of the saints. Winifred's well at Holywell is one of the Seven Wonders of Wales. The well is now covered by a lovely arched and pillared well chamber with a chapel over it, and there is a huge pool in which pilgrims bathe. Her church at Gwytherin was probably just to the south of the modern parish church, which was closed a couple of years ago and has been bought for use as a cultural and interpretative centre. It should be open on Sundays in the summer. Cadoc's monastery in Llancarfan is now a church and open to the public. It has some wonderful medieval wood carvings as well as the wall paintings. Though all these are from long after Cadoc's time, they help to remind us of the importance of the spiritual and cultural centre founded by this evil-tempered man. Villain or hero? You decide.

Further reading:
Elissa Henken, *The Welsh Saints: A Study in Patterned Lives* (1991)

2

CARATACUS:
OF LEGENDS AND LEGIONS

Ray Howell

When looking for heroes of Wales, the Home Counties may not seem the most obvious starting place. Nevertheless, it was Hertfordshire which lay at the heart of the Iron Age Catuvellauni and, on the eve of the Roman conquest, the activities of that tribe became pivotal in the historical development of Wales.

There is every indication that the Catuvellauni made difficult neighbours. They were aggressive and expansionistic, extending their territory at the expense of nearby tribes like the Atrebates. In fact, when the Atrebatic leader Verica fled to Rome, he probably provided a useful excuse for invasion. If we take into account evidence like the distribution of coins, there is every indication that one of the main leaders of Catuvellaunian expansion was a son of the powerful king Cunobelinus, Caratacus. The name is spelled in various ways: Caratacus, Caractacus or, in Welsh, Caradog. Whichever version is preferred, it is the name of a prince who became a key figure in the resistance when the Romans invaded in AD43.

INVASION

The Claudian invasion of Britain, the intervention which led to more than 350 years of Roman control, was a massive undertaking. Under the command of the general Aulus Plautius, four legions supported by auxiliary troops made up an invasion force of more than 40,000 men. One of the legions, the 2nd Augustan (which would eventually be based in Caerleon) was led by Titus Flavius Vespasianus. A quarter of a century later, he would seize the throne as the Emperor Vespasian!

Despite what must have seemed overwhelming Roman strength, there was strong native resistance. Classical writers like Cassius Dio and Cornelius Tacitus leave little doubt that the resistance was, in large part, orchestrated by Caratacus. There was a series of skirmishes in the lower Thames Valley with a major battle on the Medway. This opposition was led by Caratacus and probably his brother Togodumnus. If traditional interpretations are to be accepted, the latter was killed and eventually the resistance collapsed in the south east. Caratacus, however, was determined to carry on fighting and he moved west in an effort to attract new support. For a time, he established himself among the by-this-time divided Dubonni, possibly setting up camp on today's Minchinhampton Common in Gloucestershire.

Caratacus (or Caractacus or Caradog) addressing the Emperor in Rome

GOING WEST TO WALES

Before long, the bellicose Catuvellaunian leader moved even further west. He brought his supporters into south-east Wales and the territory of the Silures. Tacitus tells us that the Silures were warlike and powerful, and they seem to have been more than happy to accept Caratacus as a war leader and take up arms against the Romans. No doubt Caratacus was pleased to have gained such support but in doing so, he caused a re-direction of Roman troops. The whole force of the Roman military machine turned against Wales!

Recognising the need to bolster the resistance, Caratacus moved north in an attempt to link his force with the also warlike Ordovices of North Wales. The Romans were determined to prevent him from doing so. With Roman troops moving to cut off his advance, Caratacus decided, in the words of Tacitus, 'to stake his fate on a battle'. Locating the battle site has exercised the minds of archaeologists for years and we still cannot be sure where it took place. What is clear is that Caratacus chose his position carefully, taking high ground overlooking a river. Steep slopes in many places made attack difficult and where these were lacking, stone ramparts were thrown up. As the Romans advanced, we are told that 'the British chieftains went around their men, encouraging them to be unafraid'. Caratacus himself moved among his defenders explaining that this battle 'would either win back their freedom or enslave them for ever'.

Initially, the Romans hesitated but they were rallied by their commander Ostorius Scapula, the governor who had succeeded Aulus Plautius. They attacked and reached the makeshift ramparts which the defenders had erected. There, in a hail of missiles, they were forced to retreat. The Roman army, however, had a huge advantage in its ability to adjust tactics on the battlefield. In this case, they employed their *testudo* formation with its roof and walls of shields. Effectively, human tanks lumbered up the hill against Caratacus and his troops! The ploy was successful. Managing to reach the high ground, the disciplined Roman forces defeated the defenders. Although Caratacus himself escaped, among the captives were close family members, including his wife and daughter.

CAPTIVE TO ROME

Even after such a huge setback, Caratacus still tried to rally support and carry on the resistance. He fled to the north of England and the sprawling Brigantian tribal confederation. By this time, however, the Brigantes were divided and he chose the wrong faction. The Brigantian queen Cartimandua turned him over

23

to the Romans. Taken with his family and supporters as captives to Rome, their fate seemed sealed. After the inevitable 'triumphal procession' in the Roman capital, the almost inevitable outcome was death. The garrotting of the Gaulish leader Vercingetorix provided an obvious parallel.

In the event, things worked out rather differently. Caratacus made a speech in front of the Emperor himself! It must have been quite a speech. Tacitus provides us with a flavour of it:

> I had horses, men, arms, wealth. Are you surprised I am sorry to lose them? If you want to rule the world, does it follow that everyone else welcomes enslavement? If I had surrendered without a blow before being brought before you, neither my downfall nor your triumph would have become famous.

It is always prudent to be cautious in taking accounts of set-piece Roman oratory too literally. Nevertheless, whatever he said made a considerable impression. A pardon followed and Caratacus lived out the remainder of his life in Rome.

A WELSH HERO?

So does the story of Caratacus provide us with a hero of Welsh history? There can be no doubt about his obdurate resistance to Rome and he was clearly an impressive and persuasive speaker. On the other hand, he only spent a short period in what is today Wales and left behind a war zone in the tribal territories of Wales. For the Silures, the loss of their Catuvellaunian war leader seems to have had little impact. If anything, they became even more hostile after the defeat of Caratacus. They were also, at least for a time, remarkably successful.

THE SILURIAN WAR

Tacitus has given us a graphic account of the ensuing Silurian War. He explained that 'the Silures were exceptionally stubborn' as 'battle followed battle'. Many attacks were 'lightning strikes' in the woods and bogs as the Silures honed their skills at guerrilla warfare. Some engagements were major ones. As Roman forces were attempting to build forts in their territory, for example, the Silures attacked, killing the *praefectus castrorum* or senior centurion, eight other centurions and an unspecified but clearly significant number of legionary troops. Before long, a foraging party also came under attack and they were only rescued by the intervention of the cavalry. Two auxiliary units were lured into a trap; the prisoners taken were distributed to neighbouring tribes in an effort to cement alliances. As this guerrilla war dragged on, the governor, Ostorius Scapula, the conqueror of Caratacus, died. Tacitus was clear that his death was the result of exhaustion from 'his anxious responsibilities' in the war. The Silures were pleased. Tacitus tells us that 'the enemy (the Silures) exulted that so great a general, if not defeated in battle, had at least been eliminated by warfare'.

For the Romans, things went from bad to worse. A new governor was appointed but before he could arrive, the then senior military commander in Britain, Manlius Valens, attempted to defeat the Silures himself. A legion, probably the 20th, struck into Silurian territory. The Silures defeated the legion! After this startling reverse, the new governor, Aulus Gallus, decided that he could only adopt a containment strategy against the Silures who were busy plundering 'far and wide'. Tacitus was clearly incensed that the governor was content with acting 'on the defensive' against the marauding tribesmen of south-east Wales.

Despite such remarkable military successes, eventually, and many would say inevitably, the Roman military assault resumed and finally, after a quarter of a century of guerrilla warfare, the Silures were defeated. The final defeat was in AD74 or 75 when Tacitus tells us that the then governor, Julius Frontinus, 'subdued by force of arms the strong and warlike nation of the Silures, after a hard struggle, not only against the valour of his enemy, but against the difficulties of the terrain'.

The Ordovices fought on for a little longer but, in what is most accurately described as a campaign of genocide, they too were defeated by the troops of Agricola. Given the intensity of the fighting in both north and south, it is not surprising that in AD78 there were no fewer than 30,000 Roman troops in or on the borders of Wales.

CAERLEON AND CAER-WENT

After overcoming the Silures, Frontinus ordered construction of the legionary fortress of Isca, modern Caerleon, which became the headquarters of the Second Augustan legion. For decades afterwards, these troops acted as an army of occupation in the land of the Silures. Slowly new relationships between conquerors and conquered developed. Civitas administration, a form of devolved government, was eventually established in the Silurian region with the civitas capital at Venta Silurum, today's Caerwent. That development did not occur, however, until the Hadrianic period nearly half a century later.

25

Barracks and associated buildings in Caerleon, the Roman fortress of Isca

By the reign of Hadrian, who held power between 117 and 138, the passage of time had reduced the tensions which must have been high after the long Silurian War. Moreover, the Romans had other things on their minds with large numbers of troops diverted to build a rather large wall in the north of England! There is no evidence that civitas administration ever came to the Ordovices, presumably because the tribal infrastructure had been so damaged by the ruthless campaign of Agricola.

DEFEATED PEOPLES

To summarise the situation, then, the war which started with Caratacus ended in defeat with very severe social consequences. The tribes of Wales were 'defeated peoples' and were governed accordingly. So from a Welsh perspective how should we view Caratacus: as hero or villain? A case can be made for either interpretation.

The best way to try to answer the question probably lies in attempting to understand how the descendants of these resistance fighters who confronted Rome viewed the matter. For the Silures, civitas administration seems to have worked well. Affairs were managed by an *ordo* or tribal senate sitting in the curia chamber of Caerwent's basilica. Third-century inscriptions from the town confirm both the *ordo* and the survival of the tribal identity. Other finds, like a remarkable stone head associated with an altar from a fourth-century context, suggest that native tradition remained strong all through the Romano-British period.

KINGS OF GWENT

While such evidence indicates survival of native culture, our most telling clue probably comes from an even later era. As Roman control and influence waned in the late fourth and very early fifth century, the growing political vacuum was filled by the emergence of small regional kingdoms. The kingdom in at least part of the Silurian region may have grown up directly from the civitas itself. It certainly took its name from the civitas capital which by this time was being described in the vernacular, Old Welsh, as what it was assumed that it had once been – Caer Venta, the fortress of Venta, or Caer-went. Mutation led to the new kingdom being styled Gwent!

Footings of a Romano-Celtic temple in the civitas capital Venta Silurum, Caer-went

There are interesting early medieval references to kings of Gwent, one of which describes the grant of land in Caer-went to a monk named Tatheus or Tathan. The land was to be used to establish a monastery to provide *evangelica hortamenta*, evangelical exhortation, to the region. This is instructive because it indicates that the population was already Christian. It is also important in terms of assessing the legacy of Caratacus.

The land grant confirms that the decayed civitas capital retained a measure of architectural grandeur as it is described as the good, fertile, lofty, noble city of Caerwent. Similarly, it tells us important details about the kingdom. Particularly important in this respect is that the grant was made by *rex utriusque Guentonie*, the king of Gwent. The grant tells us something else as well. It names the king, giving us the earliest record we have of the name of a king of Gwent. The king was Caradoc ap Ynyr, usually called Caradog Freichfras.

The name continues to appear in the record of early medieval Wales. The man traditionally seen as the last king of Gwent who attacked and burned a hunting lodge built by Harold Godwinson in 1065, for example, shared it. He was Caradog ap Gruffudd. As we have seen, Caradog is the Welsh form of Caratacus and these early medieval records bring us back to the basic question. Caratacus was articulate, brave and obviously obsessively opposed to Rome. His stay in Wales was a short one. Nevertheless, in many ways the war leader at the beginning of the Silurian War came to personify the resistance which followed.

Despite ultimate defeat, both for Caratacus and subsequently the tribes of Wales, the stubborn resistance mounted was remarkable. That resistance seems to have retained its symbolic significance as well. Early medieval documents give us a glimpse of the early kingdoms, confirming that the name of the Catuvellaunian prince was not only remembered, it was seen as a name worthy of a king!

That is probably a good way to answer the question. An unyielding resistance to the power of Rome and a bold and articulate defence delivered to Claudius himself resonates of heroic endeavour. Never mind the Hertfordshire origins, Caratacus qualifies as a hero of Welsh history.

Further reading:
Ray Howell, *Searching for the Silures: an Iron Age Tribe in South-East Wales* (2009)

3

OWAIN AP CADWGAN: NOBLE WARRIOR OR HOMICIDAL MANIAC?

David Wyatt

Few people today are probably aware of the story of Owain ap Cadwgan, the young, violent prince of Powys who lived in the decades that straddle the year 1100. Yet during his lifetime Owain was an infamous character. His

He is one of the more colourful characters in Welsh history

Dr Kari Maund

deeds were a cause for concern at the highest levels of society and his brief existence left a blood-soaked trail worthy of any modern Tarantino movie. Yet, Owain's violent deeds had a context, and his life can reveal a great deal about the nature of society, politics and power during this momentous period in Welsh history.

DISCOVERING OWAIN – SOURCES AND PROBLEMS

Most of what we know about Owain's life and deeds is gleaned from the native Welsh chronicles and annals. Like modern newspapers, these medieval accounts provide us with reports of significant events and descriptions of the personalities of the day. As sources, they are not without their problems, not least because they were sometimes written down long after the events concerned took place. At times they are inaccurate and are often heavily biased towards certain parties. Nevertheless, for better or worse, they are the best record that we have for events in Wales in this period.

OWAIN'S WALES

In order to understand Owain's life and career we need briefly to set the scene and examine the nature of Welsh society and politics in his era. We cannot be certain but it seems likely that Owain ap Cadwgan came into the world in the late 1080s, around twenty years after the battle of Hastings. At that time, Wales was a patchwork of competing native kingdoms. There was no clear sense of Welsh unity or nationhood in this period. The Welsh political scene was violent and riven by bitter in-fighting and factional dynastic disputes for power and territory. Young men of power, like Owain, were socialised into a culture of violence and warfare. They were raised to be warriors and often lived turbulent lives focussed on raiding, plunder and the defence of their family line.

THE CULT OF THE YOUNG WARRIOR

For medieval European societies, one of the most significant rituals involved the taking of arms by young men. Following this, young men often formed into gangs or war bands and followed a riotous lifestyle. The behaviour of such war bands was significantly characterised by indiscriminate violence, the abduction of women, slave raiding and plundering activities. The Vikings' tendency towards such behaviour is pretty well known. However such practices were evident in societies across the Northern world prior to the Norman Conquest, and Wales was no exception.

THE NORMANS IN WALES

When William the Conqueror seized the throne of England, no right was granted him to rule over the Welsh kingdoms. In the aftermath of Hastings, the Normans were probably too insecure in England to worry about Wales. Welsh war bands seem to have taken advantage of this and attacked border regions with England. These attacks appear to have drawn William the Conqueror's attention to his frontier with Wales. In the late 1060s he endeavoured to do something about them.

In order to contain threats from Wales, William established a series of buffer territories or marcher earldoms and placed them under the control of tough and trusted Norman leaders. He gave these leaders wide-ranging powers which appear to have included a licence to launch individual campaigns against the Welsh kingdoms.

Since attack is the best form of defence, William's marcher earls proceeded to carve out their own lordships with some vigour over the following years. They built substantial castles at key locations and became embroiled in Welsh politics, skilfully manipulating Welsh political fragmentation in order to further their territorial aims.

Not surprisingly, Norman territorial conquests soon began to generate differences and ethnic tensions in Wales. These tensions led to periodic Welsh uprisings and resistance to the new Norman overlords. Yet, as the marcher earls gained more and more power, subsequent kings of England began to pursue a policy which also encouraged the independence of Welsh rulers.

This policy was implemented in order to maintain a balance of power between Norman and native in Wales. The result was that Welsh rulers were increasingly being drawn into the political and cultural orbit of their powerful neighbour to the east. As we shall see, this placed significant strains upon family relationships in native Welsh society.

FAMILY PROBLEMS – OWAIN AND HIS FATHER, CADWGAN

Owain's father, Cadwgan ap Bleddyn, ruled Powys from the late 1090s until his death in 1111. Cadwgan sired at least five sons but Owain appears to have been both his favourite and his recognised heir. During the 1090s, Cadwgan staunchly resisted the new Norman incomers and was heavily involved in the Welsh risings of that decade. In 1098 he fled to Ireland to escape a massive incursion into Wales by Norman forces. Yet, in the following year Cadwgan returned home and appears to have made peace with the Norman invaders and their royal ruler King Henry I.

Following his submission to the English king, Cadwgan's policy towards the Normans shifted from violence and conflict to collaboration and compromise. It is true that he became involved in a rebellious plot against Henry I in 1102, yet, his co-conspirators in this instance were not other Welsh leaders but rather the Norman nobles Robert, Earl of Shrewsbury, and his brother Arnulf of Montgomery, Earl of Pembroke.

Cadwgan was forgiven by King Henry for this misdemeanour and was subsequently given control over Ceredigion and further lands in Powys. He prospered from this co-operative attitude towards the English monarch. But his increasingly close connections with Henry and his alliances with Norman leaders in Wales appear to have created problems within his own household. This was especially true in respect of his favourite son. Owain seems to have deeply resented this intrusion of external influences into his father's court. These family tensions came to a head, as they often do, at a party!

OWAIN AND NEST – THE 'WELSH HELEN OF TROY'

In 1109, Cadwgan laid on a great feast for all of the rulers of Wales. The author of *Brut y Tywysogion* (the Welsh Chronicle of the Princes) tells us that during

Pembroke Castle

this great banquet Owain heard much talk of a beautiful Welsh noblewoman named Nest. Nest was the daughter of the Welsh ruler Rhys ap Tewdwr who had been slain by the Normans in 1093. She had subsequently been married to the powerful Norman knight Gerald of Windsor, the steward of Pembroke castle. She was also having an affair with the English king, Henry I, to whom she subsequently bore an illegitimate son also named Henry.

During Cadwgan's feast it seems that Owain learned that Gerald and Nest were staying in the nearby Norman castle at Cenarth Bychan (most probably Cilgerran castle near Cardigan). During the night that followed the banquet, Owain headed directly there. He besieged and set fire to the castle with a small band of determined young warriors. In the turmoil, Nest persuaded her husband to make a humiliating escape down the castle's latrine! The *Brut* tells us that Owain subsequently broke into the castle and raped her, before abducting her along with Gerald's children and much of his treasure.

Historians have pondered Owain's motives and actions on this pivotal night. Were these the unpredictable actions of an unpleasant personality? Was this some crime of passion? Personally, I would contest that this was no random act of youthful drunkenness and delinquency. Owain's actions must be regarded in the context of contemporary warrior codes of behaviour and honour.

From this perspective, the abduction of Nest was a deliberate symbolic statement against the Norman intrusion into Wales. Through his actions Owain was directly defying his father's will and protesting against Cadwgan's collaborative attitude towards the Normans. He was also emphasising his power by dishonouring the wife of Gerald of Windsor (and mistress of the English king) whose forces had dared to occupy Welsh territory. He did this by abducting a native

Cilgerran Castle

Welsh princess who had been sleeping with the enemy. As was often the case in early medieval societies, Owain's overtly political action was characterised by violence, plunder and female abduction.

OWAIN THE OUTLAW

Following Owain's night of violence, Cadwgan was very angry and demanded that his son should immediately return Gerald's wife and property, but to no avail. Owain was effectively outlawed and the Normans seem to have placed a bounty on his head and arranged that the war band of Madog ap Rhiddid, a sworn enemy of Owain's, should hunt down and capture the Welsh renegade. Owain appears to have learned of this plot and subsequently fled to Ireland as a fugitive.

His father, Cadwgan, appears to have felt that his inability to control his son had implicated him in Owain's crime and he accompanied him into exile. Yet, Cadwgan soon returned and submitted himself to King Henry for forgiveness. For his part, Henry appears to have followed a reconciliatory policy towards Cadwgan.

Henry rewarded the Welsh ruler's obedience with the return of his territory and also with a noble French bride. But there were significant strings attached to this favourable settlement. The author of the *Brut* relates that Cadwgan's rewards were subject to one very strict condition: that there was to be no contact between him and his son. Owain was to be banished from Powys and given no help or support of any kind. Evidently, the tensions caused by the Norman settlement were straining the very bonds between a father and his favourite son.

OWAIN AND THE *YNFYDYON* (HOT-HEADED WARRIORS)

As for Owain, he continued to act in a manner befitting the leader of a feisty Welsh war band. He returned from Ireland shortly afterwards and allied himself with those loyal to another youthful warrior, Madog ap Rhiddid, the same Madog who had once been hired by the Normans to hunt Owain down! So how had these two volatile characters been drawn together?

The author of the *Brut* notes that Madog had subsequently fallen from Norman favour because he had been harbouring and protecting a dissident band of Anglo-Saxon warriors who seem to have

...that there was to be no association or friendship between him and Owain, his son, and he was not to allow him to come into the land, and that he was not to give him either counsel or advice, either support or help.

The words of Henry I
according to the author of
Brut y Tywysogyon

33

They made for the land by night and burned it and slew all they found in it, and plundered others and took others with them in fetters and sold them to their folk or sent them bound to the ships.

Brut y Tywysogyon's account of Owain's ravages in Ceredigion in 1110

been continuing some kind of long-standing guerrilla campaign against Norman rule. The Normans had ordered Madog to hand over these English warriors but he refused and it was at this point that he struck an alliance with Owain.

What happened next is very interesting. Owain's war band joined with both Madog ap Rhiddid and the dissident Saxons and all three together carried out an orgy of ravaging and slave-raiding activities in west Wales, along with a hosting of local youths who are described as *ynfydyon*. The term *ynfydyon* is a difficult one to translate but seems to denote a group of hot–headed young warriors. Significantly, this term is used only five times by the author of the *Brut* and only in reference to Welsh warriors who attacked the Norman invaders and settlers.

The ravages of Owain's *ynfydyon* appear to have been an expression of deep-seated anxiety emanating from these young Welsh warriors. This reaction was directed against the increasing ties of allegiance between their Welsh rulers, like Owain's father, and the new Norman overlords. Furthermore, the inclusion of Anglo-Saxon warriors in Owain and Madog's unholy alliance reveals that their actions should not be regarded in terms of national resistance. Rather they were motivated by strong cultural differences with the Normans that transcended their old rivalries and ethnic divisions.

COMING IN FROM THE COLD – OWAIN AND KING HENRY I OF ENGLAND

Cadwgan's failure to control the disruptive ravages of his wayward son appears to have exasperated the king of England. However, in 1111 the issue was abruptly resolved when Cadwgan was murdered. At this juncture Henry I seems to have decided to bring Owain in from the cold and he was summoned to the royal court. The magnetism of the English monarch proved too powerful for Owain and he made peace with Henry and was granted his father's kingdom in Powys.

Following this, it appears that Henry attempted to integrate the Welsh renegade into his charmed circle. The *Brut* suggests that Henry took a personal interest in rehabilitating Owain, knighting him and taking him on an expedition to Normandy. It would seem that, like his father before him, Owain had been lured into a position of compliance. Yet, this is not quite the end of Owain's story.

34

CLASH OF THE FIREBRANDS: OWAIN AND GRUFFUDD AP RHYS

In 1115 another young firebrand prince, Gruffudd ap Rhys, returned to Wales following a long exile and began to assert his claim to power through warrior ferocity. Gruffudd adopted a strategy that consistently targeted Norman strongholds. He clearly intended to capitalise upon the tensions created by the Norman settlement. It appears that he was very successful in this respect because the author of the *Brut* remarks that following his ravages many young *ynfydyon* came to his assistance from all sides.

Henry I appears to have recognised the nature of these disruptions and he summoned the most suitable man for dealing with this troublesome character: Owain ap Cadwgan. Owain's subsequent actions reveal that he prosecuted this royal task with his trademark brutality, putting Gruffudd's men, women and children to the sword.

THE BIG PAYBACK – THE REVENGE OF GERALD OF WINDSOR

The author of the *Brut* relates that following Owain's ravages several fugitives managed to escape to the castle at Carmarthen where they found a champion in Owain's longstanding enemy, Gerald of Windsor, the husband of Nest. Gerald was probably aware of Owain's royal mission; however, unlike King Henry, he had not forgiven Owain for the rape of his wife. He, therefore, summoned a large force that surprised Owain's war band, and our man finally met with a suitably violent end being slain by the arrow fire of Flemish immigrants.

Carmarthen Castle

OWAIN AP CADWGAN; DELINQUENT OUTLAW OR WELSH HERO?

Do I regard Owain as a villain? I am not sure that we should pass moral judgements on medieval warriors but rather attempt to understand their context. Perhaps the most satisfactory way to answer that question is to look at what his contemporaries thought of him.

From the Norman perspective he was definitely a villain, a disruptive and unpredictable complication in the already complex world of Welsh politics. Native Welsh views of him may well have been more sympathetic. The author of the *Brut* clearly regarded his actions with concern

No other figure stands out among the posterity of Bleddyn with the same air of distinction and power

J E Lloyd on Owain ap Cadwgan

...dashing, but utterly irresponsible

R R Davies on Owain

but also awe. His resistance to Norman influences and his adherence to warrior values certainly seem to have earned him some begrudging admiration.

In many ways, Owain's behaviour mirrors that of the mythical Welsh anti-hero/villain Efnisien who appears in the second branch of the *Mabinogi*. Efnisien, too, was an unpredictable warrior whose actions created political problems. He too resisted external cultural influences and the dilution of Welsh blood. When we consider that the tales of the *Mabinogi* may well have first been written down during Owain's era then perhaps these similarities between medieval fiction and reality are more than just a coincidence?

POSSIBLE CHRONOLOGY

1075	Cadwgan ap Bleddyn inherits a share of Powys on his father's death
1080s?	Birth of Owain ap Cadwgan
1093	Cadwgan in open revolt against the Normans
1098	Cadwgan flees to Ireland following Norman attack
1099	Cadwgan makes peace with the Normans and English king, Henry I
1102	Cadwgan joins rebellion against Henry I with Norman earl Robert of Shrewsbury but is subsequently forgiven
1106	Owain is mentioned for the first time in the Chronicles, killing two rivals
1109	Owain rapes and abducts the Welsh princess Nest
1109	Owain is exiled and escapes to Ireland
1110	Owain returns and goes on a rampage in Ceredigion, killing and enslaving
1111	Cadwgan is murdered
1113	Owain captures and blinds his father's murderer
1114	Owain is knighted by Henry I and travels to Normandy with him
1115	Owain is killed in battle whilst on a royal mission to defeat the renegade Gruffudd ap Rhys

Further reading:

R.R. Davies *Domination and Conquest: The Experience of Ireland, Scotland and Wales, 1100–1300* (1990)

4

KNIGHTS TEMPLAR AND KNIGHTS HOSPITALLER: HEROES OR HERETICS?

Helen J. Nicholson

'Mystery', 'secret', 'hidden' – these are the words widely used in the media and popular writing to describe the Knights Templar. But the Knights Hospitaller are even more mysterious and hidden. Modern writers hardly ever mention them, except to say vaguely that they were something like the Templars. As for saying that these secret institutions were active in Wales… Well, so much rubbish has been written about these ancient groups that none of it can be true, can it? And would we want to believe that such dubious organisations had ever been at work in our country? More intriguingly, were they heroes or villains?

MYTHS AND HISTORY

There are many places in Wales which have the word 'Temple' somewhere in the name, so naturally some people claim that all these places once belonged to the Templars. The Hospitallers owned some hospices in Britain – places where poor travellers could stay and sick people were cared for – and, as there are many places in Wales called 'Ysbyty' ('hospital'), it's easy to assume that the Hospitallers owned all these places.

The Templars were destroyed after being accused of heresy, which in the Middle Ages was often linked with witchcraft. By the 16th century it had also become linked to science (Galileo was, of course, accused of heresy). Subsequently, some writers have assumed that the Templars were involved in either witchcraft or science, or in both, crediting them with introducing all sorts of secret knowledge to Britain. All in all therefore, the Templars look like villains – exotic and knowledgeable villains, but definitely villains.

Local tradition claims that this house in Bridgend belonged to the Hospitallers

The Hospitallers, on the other hand, have had a better press, even if they were abolished by King Henry VIII in 1540, after he dissolved all the monasteries in England and Wales. They were, however, re-established by Henry's daughter, Queen Mary, in 1553, only for her sister Elizabeth to let them lapse following her accession in 1558. The Hospitallers returned to favour in the 19th century, and set up the St John's Ambulance Association in 1877 to support the teaching of first aid in, among other places, the mining valleys of South Wales. This new British Order of St John also did important emergency rescue work, especially (in South Wales) when mining disasters occurred. During the First and Second World Wars, members of the Welsh St John's Ambulance Brigades volunteered for overseas ambulance and hospital work, and also performed vital emergency duties after bombing raids. Today the Order of St John in Wales is famed for its ambulance work and first aid training. These modern Hospitallers are clearly heroes, so it's natural to assume that their medieval forerunners were too.

TEMPLARS AND TEMPERANCE

19th-century industrial Wales also saw the establishment of temperance societies, in particular the so-called 'Good Templars', or 'Temlyddiaeth Dda' as they were known in Wales. 'Good Templars' was a popular title for temperance societies, partly because of the play on words between 'temperance' and 'Templar', but also because they were fighting 'a great crusade' against 'this terrible vice' of drunkenness. They urged absolute abstinence from alcohol, campaigned for prohibition, promoted education and self-help, and supported decent working conditions for working people. So, even if their medieval forebears seem villainous, the modern 'Good Templars' could certainly be viewed as heroes.

WHO WERE THE TEMPLARS AND HOSPITALLERS?

The original Hospitallers were founded in the 11th century, when the Order of the Hospital of St John of Jerusalem was set up by Italian merchants to care for poor sick pilgrims to the holy city. After the First Crusade captured Jerusalem in 1099, the hospital received generous donations from the new European settlers, who gave it property in western Europe to support its work in Palestine. In the 12th century the order began to provide military escorts for Christian pilgrims, and then military contingents to defend the land that had been conquered by the First Crusade.

The Templars began in 1120 as a small group of knights who protected Christian pilgrims on their way to and from Jerusalem, but soon took on more general military activities, just as the Hospitallers had done. The members of both institutions took lifetime monastic vows of personal poverty, chastity and obedience, and promised to help defend Christians and Christian territory against non-Christians. They won great admiration for their military discipline and played a leading role in all the crusades, but they failed to hold off Muslim military resurgence and in 1291 the last of the 'crusader states' in Syria and Palestine were conquered by the Mamluk Sultan of Egypt. From the mid-12th century the Hospitallers and Templars also played an important role in the so-called 'Reconquest' of the Iberian Peninsula, which Muslims from North Africa had largely conquered in the eighth century.

In 1307, King Philip IV of France accused the Templars of heresy. Most contemporaries who commented on the trial that followed agreed that he only attacked the Templars because he wanted their money. In 1312 Pope Clement V decided that the Order of the Temple was not proven guilty, but it had been so defamed that it could not continue. He dissolved the order and gave its property to the Hospitallers. The Hospitallers, who had by now moved their headquarters to the Greek island of Rhodes, continued to wage war against Muslims – but now by sea rather than on land. In 1530 they moved their operations to Malta, whose modern flag is still based on the Hospitallers' eight-pointed cross. In the British Isles the Hospitallers continued to run their estates until Henry VIII dissolved their Order in 1540.

WHAT DID THE TEMPLARS AND HOSPITALLERS BELIEVE?

The members of these religious institutions believed that they were serving God. Even if they never had the opportunity to go to the Holy Land and fight to protect Christians and Christian territory, they believed that simply by being a member of the institution, following its rule of life and praying for its work, they would be rewarded by God. In some places they built churches with circular naves to remind passers by – and themselves – of the circular church of the Holy Sepulchre in Jerusalem, built on the reputed site of Christ's empty tomb. It was their function, they claimed, to protect this church. They did not, however, build circular churches in Wales – in fact, there was nothing distinctive about their property in Wales.

Because the Templars' and Hospitallers' headquarters were in the Middle East, and because they consequently had frequent contact with Muslims, some commentators in the West thought that they must have been corrupted and turned against their fellow Christians, and that this was why they abandoned the Holy Land in 1291. In fact they were driven out by the Muslims' superior military forces.

There is no sign that the Templars and Hospitallers in Wales believed anything out of the ordinary, or that they lived strange lives. When the Templars across Europe were arrested in 1307 and 1308, charged with worshipping idols and other heretical activities, all their property was confiscated and valued, but no idols were found, or indeed any other sign of heresy. In fact, the Templars' churches had fine statues of the saints, decorative containers of holy relics and many copies of service books, just like other churches of the time. It seems that the Templars' beliefs were just the same as other Christians in Europe. So, nothing villainous here.

HOW DID THEY COME TO WALES?

The Templars and Hospitallers were given property in Wales by landowners who wanted to support their work in the Holy Land, but who could not risk or afford to go on crusade themselves. The Templars were the best known for their involvement in the crusades, but they did not receive many gifts of land within Wales. Although there are several places in Wales with the name 'Temple', in fact most of these names either refer to prehistoric monuments or are modern. In 1156 the Countess of Warwick gave the Templars the church of Llanmadoc in Gower, and until the early 1280s they held Templeton in Pembrokeshire – contemporary documents call it *villa Templar*, 'Templars' village'. The famous William Marshal may also have given them the mill they owned outside Pembroke castle, and may have been the donor who gave them the church of Kemeys Commander on the River Usk. The Templars were also given small parcels of land in

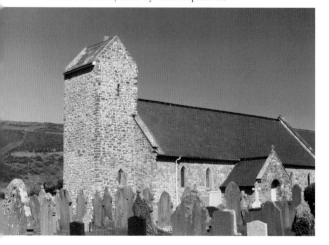
Rhossili church, built by the Hospitallers

Glamorganshire and Gwent. But although the Templars received extensive properties in the Welsh March territories of Herefordshire and Shropshire, the Welsh themselves did not make donations to them.

In contrast, the Welsh in Pembrokeshire and Gwynedd did donate to the Hospitallers. The Hospitallers' house at Slebech on the Eastern Cleddau river was given to them by a Flemish family who had settled in the area, and was supported by donations from Normans, Welsh and English alike.

SLEBECH STRONGHOLD

Slebech became an administrative centre or commandery, the Hospitallers' fourth richest commandery in England and Wales. In 1535, when King Henry VIII began dissolving the monasteries, Slebech was the third richest religious house in Wales – surpassed only by the famous monasteries of Tintern and Valle Crucis.

In Ceredigion, the Norman noble Roger de Clare gave the Hospitallers Ystradmeurig after he recaptured the land from the Welsh in 1158. When the Welsh prince Lord Rhys of Deheubarth won it back in 1164, he enlarged de Clare's gift to the Hospitallers. In Gwynedd, in the heart of Welsh Wales, the Hospitallers had a church and a hospice for travellers at Dolgynwal on the River Conwy. This may have been supported by Prince Llywelyn ap Iorwerth 'the Great'. The hospice was burned down in the early 15th century during Owain Glyndŵr's revolt, but the church survived. The little town here is now called Ysbyty Ifan after the Hospitallers. The Hospitallers also had land at Gwanas, near Dolgellau. They also received many gifts of land and churches in Glamorganshire, including most of the parish churches in the Gower peninsula, entrusted to their care by the local Norman landlords.

Heroes or villains? The Templars' heroic deeds in the Middle East don't seem to have particularly impressed most people in Wales, whether Norman or Welsh; perhaps the fact that in the 12th and early 13th centuries they

The church tower at Slebech

41

were highly trusted servants of the kings of England didn't help their cause in Wales. So they did not receive many gifts of land in Wales. The Hospitallers, on the other hand, were far more involved in the life of Wales, providing accommodation for pilgrims and other poor travellers.

Templars on Don Felipe's tomb, at Villalcázar de Sirga in Spain

WHAT DID THE TEMPLARS AND HOSPITALLERS DO IN WALES?

Ysbyty Ifan

The main function of the Templars' and Hospitallers' properties in western Europe was to raise money and recruits for their operations in the Middle East. As a result of this, they also became involved in local life. They had to ensure that some of their income was put aside for repairs to the parish churches entrusted to them, and appoint suitable priests to these churches. They employed local people on their estates. The Hospitallers owned the hospice at Ysbyty Ifan, which provided accommodation for travellers on the road to Conwy. They may also have provided accommodation at Gwanas – on the main road south from Dolgellau – and at Ystradmeurig, close to the popular pilgrim destination of Strata Florida.

Slebech in particular had to cater for a large number of travellers, as it was on a pilgrim route to St David's. In 1338 the Hospitallers at Slebech complained to their headquarters on Rhodes about the excessive expense caused by the large number of travellers who flocked there seeking accommodation. The problem got worse: by the early 15th century so many people wanted to cross the river here that a causeway was proposed across the Eastern Cleddau, and in 1419 the Hospitallers obtained the Pope's permission to collect charitable donations for the scheme. It is not clear whether the causeway was built, but local people have said that at low tide it is, or was, possible to ford the river here across a stony track named Lammas Ford, so perhaps this was the causeway which the Hospitallers constructed. By the mid-15th century the Welsh Hospitallers were famous for their hospitality, which was praised by the Welsh poets Lewys Glyn Cothi and Dafydd Nanmor. Locally, then, they were heroes.

BUT, WAIT A MOMENT – DIDN'T THEY FIGHT AS WELL?

Generally both the Templars and the Hospitallers tried to keep out of local warfare. It was all too easy to fritter away on local skirmishes the money they had collected to help Christians in the Middle East. In 1338 the Hospitallers in Wales told their headquarters on Rhodes that, far from fighting in Wales, they were paying local nobles and officials to protect them against their enemies and keep the peace.

But this was half a century after King Edward I's conquest of Wales. Edward I had thought very highly of both the Templars and Hospitallers – he had been on crusade to the Holy Land and so he had seen their forces in action on their home ground. However, as king, he expected his friends to earn their keep, and he expected the Templars and Hospitallers to fight for him at home as well as fighting for Christendom overseas. The lieutenant-commander of the Templars in England may have been involved in Edward I's military action against Llywelyn ap Gruffudd in May 1282. The Hospitaller commander in North Wales was reimbursed during the winter of 1294–95 for paying a force of infantry stationed in Meirionnydd. Apparently he had been involved with one of Edward's Welsh allies in putting down the Welsh rebellion at that time.

HEROES OR VILLAINS?

Were the Templars and Hospitallers villains for the Welsh? It would have been very difficult for them to say 'no' to King Edward I. They relied on him to protect their interests and allow them to export money, men and equipment out of Britain to the Middle East, and they were hoping that he would organise another crusade to win back the Christian holy sites. And Edward I was not the sort of king who would take 'no' for an answer. Probably the people of Wales were right not to give the Templars much property in Wales because, when the going got tough, the Templars would always side with the king of England. That doesn't make them out-and-out villains, but we can say that they never really got involved in Wales.

The Hospitallers were another matter. They were part of Welsh society, winning praise from the Welsh poets, and – although they didn't own all the places called 'Ysbyty' – caring for travellers. Their widespread estates meant that they had vested interests in Wales. Although they supported King Edward I's military operations, they also allied with local gentry to help keep the peace. Their caring legacy survives in the work of St John's Ambulance, so perhaps we might allow them to be heroes.

Further reading:
Kathryn Hurlock, *Wales and the Crusades, c. 1095–1291* (2011)

5

GERALD OF WALES: WELSH PATRIOT OR ENGLISH IMPERIALIST?

Richard Marsden

In a 2004 poll of Wales's greatest heroes, the late 12th-century churchman and writer Gerald of Wales (1146–1223) ranked 85th. The eclectic trinity of Aneurin Bevan, Owain Glyndŵr and Tom Jones occupied the top three spots. Whilst Gerald's place in Wales's popular consciousness cannot compete with such celebrated figures, the fact that he featured on the list at all is telling. Gerald is evidently seen, by some at least, as a hero of Welsh history.

Tomb of the Lord Rhys at St David's Cathedral

On the face of it this seems perfectly reasonable. Gerald was born in Pembrokeshire and spent his childhood there. Although his father was Norman he was, in part at least, descended from Welsh stock and could boast familial links with Rhys ap Gruffudd, warrior-king of south-west Wales. He was thus arguably Welsh by blood and Welsh by birth.

Having taken holy orders at a young age, Gerald pursued a career within the Welsh church. In the mid 1170s he was appointed Archdeacon of Brecon and later administered the diocese of St David's on behalf of an absent bishop. He also wrote a number of lively and readable books containing a wealth of information on Welsh life and society in the Middle Ages.

In particular, Gerald's reputation as a Welsh patriot is based on his efforts to have St David's recognised as an archbishopric. Had he been successful the Welsh church would have been liberated from the allegiance which, in this period, it owed to the archbishopric of Canterbury in England.

Moreover, during the 12th century this English ecclesiastical overlordship was matched by political dominance. Norman lords took chunks of Wales for their own and English kings mounted frequent expeditions against the remaining Welsh rulers. In this context it is difficult not to see Gerald's championing of the Welsh church in patriotic terms.

THE STRUGGLE FOR ST DAVID'S

Based on the facts outlined above, Gerald does indeed appear to be a Welshman through and through; fighting the religious oppression of the hated *Sais* at a time when they were encroaching further and further into the heartlands of Wales.

This view is supported by the praise that he heaped upon his compatriots. In his writings he lauded their martial skills and courage in battle, highlighted their generous and hospitable natures, emphasised their intellectual capacities, wit and prowess in debate, and extolled their musical abilities. Furthermore, he was at pains to emphasise his own Welsh roots in his autobiography. These certainly seem to be the attitudes of a man who was proud of his Welsh heritage.

The opening sally of the struggle for St David's occurred in 1176 when the incumbent bishop died. The cathedral chapter, who theoretically at least had the power to elect the next bishop, chose Gerald as his successor. However, theory and practice were often a long way apart during the Middle Ages. In reality, kings tended to control the appointment of bishops through the simple expedient of having the biggest stick.

The cathedral chapter therefore sought approval for their decision from Henry II of England. Unfortunately for Gerald, Henry refused to accept his nomination and installed his own Norman favourite as bishop instead. With his hopes dashed, Gerald retreated into his books.

Evidently the politically-savvy Henry was unwilling to allow a Welsh candidate, who could claim kinship with a leading Welsh prince, to be appointed to the country's most prestigious bishopric. His concern was that

St David's Cathedral and Bishop's Palace

this would give the Welsh a standard around which to rally in defiance of English power. As Gerald himself later put it, 'of the three archbishoprics, that of our church is found in the texts of our histories to be third in number, but first in position'. In this way he claimed for St David's a prestige greater even than that of Canterbury.

As this quotation shows, Gerald was committed to establishing St David's as an archbishopric and releasing the Welsh church from its subordination to Canterbury. That commitment was demonstrated by the fact that he was subsequently offered the bishoprics of Bangor and Llandaf, but turned them down because of his belief in the St David's cause.

His second chance came in 1198 with the death of the bishop whom Henry had appointed to St David's in 1176. Gerald again had the backing of the cathedral chapter but was this time opposed by the Archbishop of Canterbury, who feared the loss of power that an independent Welsh church would spell. Nevertheless, in 1199 the Chapter elected Gerald bishop on the understanding that he would petition the Pope to make St David's an archbishopric.

Between 1199 and 1203, Gerald did all he could to attain that goal. He called upon every ally and used up every favour at his disposal, took no fewer than three trips to Rome to see the Pope, was put on trial by enemies in England for stirring up Welsh rebellion, and incurred heavy personal debt.

Yet it was to no avail. Eventually even his Welsh supporters deserted him for fear of English reprisals, and in 1203 Gerald was forced to admit defeat. He was compelled to relinquish his claim to St David's, resign as Archdeacon of Brecon, and go into embittered retirement. The dream of a sovereign Welsh church was over.

GERALD THE WELSHMAN

This story of aspiration and defeat seems like an apt symbol for Wales's wider struggle against England over the past thousand years. This is certainly the light in which many more recent Welsh writers and historians have seen Gerald.

For example, a biography of Gerald published in 1889 by the Welsh antiquary Henry Owen was called 'Gerald the Welshman'. This title unambiguously presented its subject as Welsh by birth, blood and culture. Within it, Owen referred to Gerald as a 'patriotic Welshman' and characterised his efforts regarding St David's as a battle for 'the honour of Wales'.

The influential Welsh historian John Edward Lloyd saw Gerald in similar terms. Writing in 1911, he portrayed him as 'never failing to emphasize his

If there was more of Norman than of Welsh blood in his veins it was the Welsh blood that ran the thicker.

Professor Thomas Jones on the power of Gerald's Welsh lineage

Welsh descent, regarding Wales as his beloved fatherland, and posing as a Welsh patriotic leader'. Reading this quotation in isolation, you could be forgiven for thinking that Gerald was the Ieuan Wyn Jones of his day.

This interpretation was taken further by Professor Thomas Jones of Aberystwyth University. In 1947 Jones produced another biography of Gerald, also entitled 'Gerald the Welshman'. This work had an even more nationalistic flavour than its predecessor, and summarised Gerald's life as follows: 'it was in Wales that he was born, in Wales that he spent the greater part of his life, it was for the church of Wales that he fought so courageously; Wales and the life of her people form the subject of the majority of his books; and it is in the soil of Wales that he found his last resting place.'

As far as these historians were concerned, Gerald's background and his efforts on behalf of the Welsh church demonstrated conclusively that his loyalties lay with Wales rather than England.

THE ENGLISH CONNECTION

The evidence above does seem to imply that Gerald was a champion of Welsh freedom against English oppression. Furthermore, several eminent historians have appeared over the years as expert witnesses in support of that interpretation.

As is often the case with history, however, appearances can be deceptive. The Gerald that we have seen so far is only part of the story; it is just as easy to view him as an agent of English imperialism.

For starters, he was only one quarter Welsh. The rest of his lineage was unmistakably Norman and he was part of the top echelon of Norman society in Wales. Moreover, the lands held by his father and numerous Norman relations had been taken from the Welsh by force only a few decades before he was born.

Furthermore, his career was intimately associated with the English church. Between 1174 and 1176 he was employed as a direct representative of Canterbury in Wales. In 1189, meanwhile, he accompanied the Archbishop of Canterbury on a tour of his homeland, exhorting Welsh and Normans alike to go on crusade. Gerald's relationship with the English church was therefore rather closer than is allowed by the nationalist perspective put forward above.

Gerald also had powerful links with the English monarchy. Despite his previous refusal to appoint Gerald Bishop of St David's, by 1184 Henry II's attitude had mellowed. In that year the king took Gerald on as a royal clerk, a position that would put him at the heart of English affairs for the next twelve years. Indeed, it was in that role that Gerald served as Henry's envoy to various Welsh kings in the early 1190s.

Manorbier Castle

Even when he retired from court under something of a cloud in 1196, it was to Lincoln that Gerald went rather than his archdeaconry of Brecon or his childhood home of Pembrokeshire. These do not seem to be the actions of a man whose very reason for being was the liberation of Wales from foreign oppression.

So Gerald was, for a significant chunk of his life, politically aligned with the English church and the English monarchy. Such connections throw severe doubt on a simplistically nationalistic interpretation of his career.

We also need to remember that Gerald was only human. Whilst he was undoubtedly gifted, intelligent, resourceful and determined, his writings also suggest that he was vain, self-aggrandising and occasionally self-delusional. This was a man who wrote his own autobiography anonymously and in the third-person, missing no opportunity to extol his own virtues. It has also been suggested that he only returned to the St David's cause at the end of the 12th century after trying and failing to be appointed to a wealthy bishopric in England.

Bearing this in mind, could it be that Gerald's efforts to become leader of an independent Welsh church were, to an extent at least, motivated by personal ambition and an over-inflated ego?

CIVILISING THE BARBARIANS

Yet Gerald was a churchman and therefore answerable to a higher power than his Welsh blood, the English monarchy, or even his own ambitions. Many of his opinions and actions were ideologically motivated by a religious outlook which mirrored that of church leaders in England.

Gerald was a product of what historians call the 'Reform Church'. This was an ecclesiastical movement of the 11th and 12th centuries which sought to re-orientate the moral compass of society. Within the church, priestly marriage was a particular source of consternation, whilst in wider society it

It was because of their sins, and more particularly the wicked and detestable vice of homosexuality, that the Welsh were punished by God.

Gerald explaining why the Welsh lost most of Britain to the English

was again sex and marriage that formed the focus of the reformers' zeal.

These reform ideas were already well established in England, having been brought to the kingdom through the Norman Conquest a century before. Gerald was introduced to them during his early education in Norman-occupied Pembrokeshire and then Gloucester. He was further instilled with them when, as a young man, he studied and later taught in the church schools of Paris, a centre of reform ideology.

It must have been a shock for him to return to Wales at the start of the 1170s. Society and church in most of Wales were rather different from the ideals that reformers like Gerald cherished. In Wales, priests habitually married and had children. In addition, it was common practice for nobles to keep concubines, for couples to co-habit before matrimony, and for cousins to marry one another.

Such practices were anathema to Gerald and he reported them in sensationalist terms in his writings. Indeed, his works betray a kind of horrified fascination with all things sexual, which perhaps stemmed in part from his own priestly celibacy. At one point, for instance, he stated that 'incest is extremely common among the Welsh, both in the lower classes and the better educated people'.

Gerald also condemned other aspects of Welsh life, asserting that 'it is the habit of the Welsh to steal anything they can lay their hands on and to live on plunder, theft and robbery'. He then highlighted what he saw as their relentless desire to acquire land and possessions, writing that 'quarrels and lawsuits result, murders and arsons, not to mention frequent fratricides'. Elsewhere he commented on the lawlessness and political instability of the remaining Welsh kingdoms.

In this way Gerald painted a picture of the Welsh as immoral, irreligious barbarians in need of a civilising influence from England. In this he was like a 19th-century missionary intent on bringing civilisation and salvation to the heathen savages. Like many of his contemporaries across the border, he believed that it was his duty to bring moral order to Welsh society.

Gerald's religious beliefs made him every inch the Norman churchman. In addition he was employed for years by the English state and the English church, both of which were intent on maintaining and extending English power in Wales. Taken in conjunction with his Norman parentage, is this really the profile of a Welsh patriot?

IN SEARCH OF GERALD

In truth Gerald was neither patriot nor imperialist as we understand the terms today. His actions and writings contained elements of both, but he was far too complex a figure to fit into such crude pigeon-holes.

That complexity came through clearly in one of his letters to the Pope. In it he wrote, 'I am descended from both nations, from the Princes of Wales and from the Barons of the March, who defend the boundaries of the realm against the continual rebellion of the Welsh, and yet I hate injustice by whichever nation it be committed'. As the quotation implies, Gerald was neither fully Welsh nor properly English but had powerful affinities with both.

This is also shown in one of his books, in which he suggested how the English might conquer Wales once and for all. Yet in the very next chapter he advised the Welsh on how they could best go about resisting that conquest.

It is certainly possible to see Gerald a hero of Welsh history, fighting the good fight against English tyranny. He can also be viewed as a tool of that tyranny, contributing to the slow conquest of Wales by its larger neighbour. However, in reality neither of these labels is particularly applicable, weighed down as they are by the baggage of modern nationalism. Could it be that in viewing Gerald through the lens of the present we are missing out on what made him special in his own day?

Perhaps instead Wales can today be proud of Gerald for what he was; an accomplished intellectual, a lively and observant writer, a determined adversary, a witness to many of the key events of the period, and very much a product of his own time. Whilst that may not justify the number one spot in a poll of Welsh heroes, number 85 seems just about right.

CHRONOLOGY OF GERALD'S LIFE

1146 Born at Manorbier in Pembrokeshire
1160s Educated in the ecclesiastical schools of Paris
1174 Appointed Archdeacon of Brecon
1176 Tried and failed to be appointed Bishop of St David's
1180 Began administering the bishopric of St David's in the bishop's absence
1184 Taken on as a royal clerk by King Henry II of England
1188 Accompanied the Archbishop of Canterbury on a journey around Wales
1196 Retired from the English royal court and went to live in Lincoln
1198-1203 Tried and failed to have St David's raised to an archbishopric with himself as the first archbishop
1223 Died in Hereford after a long retirement in Lincoln

Further reading:
R. Bartlett, *Gerald of Wales: A Voice of the Middle Ages* (2nd ed., 2006)

51

6

KATHERYN OF BERAIN: MURDERESS OR PATRONESS?

Katharine K. Olson

On the surface, her story has all the elements of a lurid modern romance. A young, beautiful gentlewoman from North Wales, connected by blood and marriage to some of Wales's most influential families – and perhaps the Tudors – marries four times, and outlives three of her husbands. Did this wealthy heiress poison her husbands with her own hand, and kill a succession of lovers? Did she callously agree to marry her second husband on the way to the funeral of her first? Was Katheryn of Berain a 16th-century villainess?

Or, perhaps, has she simply been the victim of spiteful gossip, folk stories, and centuries of exaggeration? Should she rightly be seen instead as a dedicated wife, mother, bardic patron, and indeed a 16th-century heroine – the original *Mam Cymru* ('mother of Wales')?

BIRTH AND ANCESTRY: TUDOR ROYAL BLOOD?

Katheryn was probably born around 1540, at Berain in Llanefydd (Denbighshire). Her parents were of noble blood. Katheryn's father was Tudur ap Robert Fychan, a courtier and soldier praised by a contemporary poet for his wisdom. Siôn Tudur wrote how Katheryn's father was descended from very esteemed ancestors, including the ancient line of Heilin Frych – indeed, it was even claimed subsequently that he descended from the founder of one of the so-called noble tribes of Wales.

Yet it is her mother's ancestry that has drawn the most attention. Her mother, Jane, was the daughter of Sir Roland Velville (d.1535), while her maternal grandmother, Agnes, was the daughter of Sir William Gruffudd of Penrhyn, the head of one of the most powerful gentry families in Tudor Gwynedd.

Beaumaris Castle

The Velville connection was key. Velville was allegedly the illegitimate son of Henry VII, or Henry Tudor, whose victory at the Battle of Bosworth Field in 1485 saw the accession of the Tudor dynasty to the throne. According to the story, Henry VII had impregnated a Breton lady whilst in exile in Brittany waiting for his chance to gain the throne. Velville was shown some royal favour – knighted during the reign of Henry VII, and later given lands in Anglesey and the position of Constable of Beaumaris Castle there.

Whether this was true, we will likely never know for certain. Short of DNA testing or the discovery of lost historical documents, all historians can do is speculate based on the available evidence. As far as we know, no account which conclusively settles the matter or points out a physical or familial resemblance between Sir Roland de Velville and Henry VII or Henry VIII has survived from Velville's lifetime. However, one later commentator (in Harley MS. 1971) did remark on a physical similarity between Henry VIII and Velville. Apparently both were distinguished by their height, strength, and fair colouring.

While it is possible that Velville may have been an illegitimate son of Henry VII, it is also feasible he was merely a courtier who won royal favour for entirely different reasons, as has been argued by historians in the past.

Whatever the truth, it is clear that the supposed royal origins of Katheryn's grandfather were readily believed by the Welsh poets in the 16th century, whose poetry constitutes a very important historical and genealogical source. Many sang of how he sprang from a line of royal blood. When Velville died in 1535, the poet Dafydd Alaw praised him as having been descended from the legendary early British king Brutus, and noted also that he came from a line of kings and had the blood of earls in his veins.

KATHERYN THE QUEEN'S COUSIN

The idea that Katheryn was of Tudor royal blood, the Duke of Brittany's son, and the cousin of Elizabeth I persisted for years to come within bardic circles. A collection of poetry in honour of Katheryn's family (Christ Church MS. 184) contains a number of poems which allude to the royal origins of her family. The poet Wiliam Cynwal declared that Katheryn's son, John Salisbury, came from a line 'of the blood of kings', and also 'the earls of all England', for example.

KATHERYN'S EARLY LIFE AND FIRST MARRIAGE

Katheryn's mother died when Katheryn was a child, and her father remarried, and had more children. He lived until Katheryn was likely in her twenties, dying in 1564.

But well before his death, Katheryn had already left the family home. By 1558 she had been living at the estate of the powerful Salisbury family of Lleweni (Denbighshire) for some time, growing accustomed to life there.

There was a simple reason for this move: she was to marry John Salisbury (c.1542–1566), who was the son and heir of Sir John Salisbury, the owner of Lleweni. They had likely been promised in marriage for some time as children, but it was only in 1558 that they were formally married.

Katheryn and John had two sons together: Thomas and John Salisbury. Thomas, the eldest, was ultimately to die before Katheryn, caught up in the high politics of the day. He was found guilty of high treason for his part in the so-called Babington Plot to reinstate Catholicism as the official religion by assassinating Queen Elizabeth I (a Protestant) and putting Mary, Queen of Scots (a Catholic), on the throne in her place. He was executed in London in 1586. Katheryn's marriage to John Salisbury, however, was a short one. He appears to have hastily made a will in May 1566, and died at Berain by mid-July at the latest.

By 1566 too, Katheryn's father was dead, and as she was her parents' only surviving child, she stood to inherit a sizeable sum in money and lands. In addition to approximately 1,000 acres of land on Anglesey, the Berain estate itself equalled some 3,000 acres, and meant substantial income of some £300 a year in rentals.

The Coach House, Lleweni Hall, photographed in 1997. Lleweni was once the Denbighshire home of the Salisbury family

SECOND MARRIAGE

As a young widow of noble (perhaps royal) blood and still of child-bearing years and heiress to a substantial landed estate, Katheryn was quite a catch. It comes as no surprise, then, that less than a year later (in 1567), she had married again. Her new husband was Sir Richard Clough of Denbigh (d.1570). His family had risen to wealth and status through his father's success in trade as a Denbigh glover, and fortunate marriages. Richard Clough himself achieved great wealth and status as a merchant and agent of the English crown in international trade in Europe.

Clough arrived on a visit home to Wales in April 1567, and less than three weeks later he had married Katheryn. Her two sons from her first marriage stayed with their grandparents, and the newlyweds promptly departed for London and then journeyed to Antwerp, where they settled until 1569, when Clough moved to Hamburg. Katheryn had two more children with Clough, both daughters: Ann (1568) and Mary (1570).

Katheryn's marriage to Clough, however, was destined to be her shortest. He died in 1570 in Hamburg. He appears to have died of what has been described as a 'lingering sickness' which involved insomnia and headaches amongst other symptoms.

BARDIC PATRONAGE AND THIRD MARRIAGE

It was roughly three years before Katheryn married again, but she was not short of proposals in the interim. Her potential suitors included John Vaughan of Golden Grove (Carmarthenshire), whom she refused. Meanwhile, she seems to have returned to her native North Wales, and settled at Berain, where she focused on family matters, and acted as a patron of the native Welsh poets.

She commissioned a collection of poetry in honour of her family (related both by blood and marriage) from the poet Wiliam Cynwal. This survives today in Christ Church College, Oxford. It contains poems about Katheryn, Clough, the Salisburies, and a variety of other extended family. Katheryn herself was welcomed back from the continent most warmly, and Cynwal sings of her supposed descent from Brutus, Aeneas, biblical personages, and Roman gods, ultimately tracing her ancestry back to Adam and even God himself. Producing such a legendary genealogy for members of the Welsh gentry was not at all uncommon.

Ultimately, she followed the advice given in another of Cynwal's poems in honour of her, and married again. Her third husband was Maurice Wynn (d.1580) of the powerful Gwydir family based by Llanrwst in Caernarfonshire, to whom she was married by early 1573. A year later, her first-born son, Thomas Salisbury, was married to Maurice Wynn's daughter Margaret (from a previous marriage). This was a common enough arrangement at a time when a widow and a widower of wealth and status remarried.

'A WOMAN, FOOLISH AND FOND'

A letter penned by Katheryn during this marriage survives. In 1576/1577 she wrote to her stepson John Wynn of Gwydir (who was residing in London). Katheryn refers to herself as 'a woman, foolish and fond' and asks him to advise her, as a servant and relative of hers was in trouble for a murder. She makes an emotional appeal for help, saying that her son Thomas Salisbury (now his brother-in-law) was especially attached to the accused man, and loved him greatly.

Katheryn and Maurice Wynn had two children: a son, Edward, and a daughter, Jane. But after more than seven years of marriage, Maurice Wynn died in August 1580. Once again, Katheryn was a widow.

FOURTH MARRIAGE AND DEATH

After Maurice Wynn's death, Katheryn left Gwydir and returned to her ancestral home of Berain. She lived there with many of her children, and her daughter-in-law Margaret (Wynn).

But by January 1583, she was married again, for a fourth and final time. Her new husband was Edward Thelwall (d.1610) of Plas-y-Ward in Denbighshire. Thelwall's son was married to her daughter Jane at the same time. The newlyweds did not move from Berain, however, until 1586. Nor did they have children: Katheryn's child-bearing days were over.

Katheryn's final husband outlived her. She died on August 27, 1591, at Thelwall's estate of Plas-y-Ward. She was still fairly young: around fifty years old. It is not clear how she died.

On September 1, 1591, Katheryn was buried in Llanefydd parish church. As she had been a patron of the native Welsh poets, many of them wrote elegies at her death. Siôn Tudur, for example, praised her as a fair heiress of great estate who had made choice marriages, exclaiming on the greatness of her ancestors and her great generosity. He claimed that with her death God had taken his very soul and expressed the hope that Katheryn now resided in heaven. She was praised by other poets for her patronage, her generosity in providing food, drink, and clothes to the poets, her virtue, her beauty, her ancestry, the nobility of her husbands and marriages, and much more. These poems in her honour ensured that Katheryn's story lived on.

LATER STORIES AND TRADITIONS ABOUT KATHERYN

Indeed, Katheryn's story did not fail to interest antiquarians and tourists in the 18th and 19th centuries either, and gave rise to some distinctly suspect claims and exaggerations.

Her Tudor ancestry went unmentioned by John Davies, the Llansilin antiquary, in his *A Display of Herauldry* (1716). However, the Flintshire antiquarian Thomas Pennant (1726–1798), who went on a number of tours of Wales in the early 1770s and recorded these in great detail, had much to say about Katheryn and her story. He wrote that Sir Roland Velville was the 'reputed base son of Henry VII' – referring to Katheryn's supposed Tudor ancestry.

Pennant also recorded a local tradition that had grown up about Katheryn's second marriage. After the death of her first husband, Sir John Salisbury, Sir Richard Clough proposed to her while the pair were on their way to the church for Salisbury's funeral. No sooner was the service over than Maurice

Wynn of Gwydir also proposed – he was turned down, but with the promise that if Katheryn were to be made a widow again, she would accept.

Modern scholars, however, have shown this story to be untrue. The events in it are borrowed from a popular tale of the time, and later became attached to Katheryn.

Pennant wrote too that Katheryn kept some of the hair of her second husband, Sir Richard Clough, after his death, as he was her favourite out of all her husbands. What Katheryn's true feelings were on the matter, however, we simply don't know.

KATHERYN THE PROLIFIC

Stories about Katheryn abounded. When Jinny Jenks of Enfield went on a tour of North Wales in the summer of 1772, she saw a fine portrait of Katheryn during the trip – she 'by whom all the Welch became related, and from whom every Family chuses to trace their Pedigrees, she having Nine Husbands and a Child by each'. By this time, the number of Katheryn's husbands and children had clearly undergone some embellishment!

Thomas Nicholas, writing in 1872 about the county families of Wales, noted that Katheryn was 'the most noted of her race in this county', a woman who had 'married four husbands, each of a high and honourable house, and had such a numerous offspring that the name was given her of *Mam Cymru,* "the mother of Wales."' He also claimed that Katheryn's father, Tudur ap Robert, was descended directly (ninth in line) from Marchweithian, Lord of Isaled, and supposedly responsible for founding the eleventh noble tribe of Wales. Indeed, looking at a copy of her portrait, he came to the conclusion she was 'a person of firmness and intelligence, and these qualities, added to her estate and numerous alliances and offspring, supplied her with a charm which the bardic heralds [poets/genealogists] of the time knew not how to resist; they spared her no pains, accordingly, to provide her with a [great and ancient] lineage' – all the way back to the legendary early kings of Britain!

Other malicious stories about Katheryn also grew up. She was said to have had a variety of lovers in addition to her husbands. When she wished to rid herself of a lover, she allegedly would pour molten lead into his ears as he slept, and then bury the body in the extensive orchards at Berain.

KATHERYN OF BERAIN: HER LEGACY

In 1929, John Ballinger wrote that Katheryn's story formed the basis of 'one of the chief romances of North Wales'. And four centuries years after her death, the life, ancestry, and husbands of Katheryn of Berain, or Catrin o Ferain as she is known in Welsh, continue to fascinate. Over time, Katheryn's story has been embroidered and exaggerated, but it remains recognizably hers. She did not fade into the background, or come to be forgotten, like so many women in Tudor Wales.

As daughter, wife, and mother to some of North Wales's most influential gentry families, Katheryn is fortunate in that her story has endured – due likely to her status (and that of her descendants), as well as the story's nature. Her supposed genealogy (particularly the alleged link to Henry Tudor) has also remained a matter for debate. Likewise, a range of historical documents concerning her and written by her have survived, as well as at least one contemporary portrait, painted in 1568 by Adrien van Cronenburg.

Katheryn of Berain, as painted by Adrien van Cronenburg

Beyond her status and genealogy, her story of four husbands, three of whom she buried, continues to intrigue. For a woman today to divorce three or four times is not unheard of, but for three of her four husbands to predecease her suggests some possible wrongdoing on Katheryn's part to modern audiences. It has indeed been suggested that she poisoned her husbands and killed numerous lovers, but there is absolutely no evidence for this.

It was in fact usual for people in the 16th century to die suddenly or young. The health and hygiene provisions that we take for granted today were absent. People could die for seemingly trivial reasons, from food poisoning to routine sicknesses like a cold or other infection, and clean water, decent food, sanitation, and medical care were major problems. People's lifespans were accordingly shorter.

So why has this image of Katheryn as a villainess not disappeared? The cause may lie in the perception that Katheryn was an independent woman and seductress or *femme fatale* in the modern sense, making all her own decisions, captivating and choosing her husbands in turn, bending them to her will, and discarding them.

But while she enjoyed great wealth and status, it is also true that Katheryn spent much of her life in the traditional roles of both wife and mother to her six children.

Yet she was actively engaged too in business affairs, wrote letters, and was also a patron of the native Welsh poets, commissioning a collection of verse in honour of her family.

Katheryn's many children and their influential descendants form another important part of her legacy as a mother. But she was not, however, unique in her large family. Many women of the time had even more children than Katheryn, but giving birth to a succession of healthy children that all reached adulthood was far less easy than it is today. Indeed, it was not unusual for women to die in childbirth or sicken and die afterwards (in 1537, even Jane Seymour – Henry VIII's third wife – died in this way). Welsh records of this period are full of tragic stories about the number of infants who were stillborn or died in infancy or as children due to a variety of illnesses and ailments.

Katheryn was, then, a fortunate mother, and a very remarkable, but not entirely unique woman in her own right. So while her epithet *Mam Cymru* may be overstepping the mark, it speaks of her success in this role and others. While not the original Welsh *mam*, she certainly was a memorable woman – and both her story and legacy (in the form of her many descendants) live on today.

Further reading:
J. Ballinger, 'Katheryn of Berain', *Y Cymmrodor*, 40 (1929), pp.1–42

7

OLIVER CROMWELL: GOD'S ENGLISHMAN OR RED DRAGON?

Lloyd Bowen

Oliver Cromwell has never been a figure around whom a cosy consensus could form. He was the devious Machiavelli behind the execution of Charles I in 1649; the dictator who ruled as Lord Protector during Britain's brief flirtation with republicanism; the butcher of Drogheda and Wexford. Alternatively, he was the far-sighted politician whose bold revolution fatally undermined the power of the monarchy and set the country on the road to a modern constitution; the humble champion of individual liberties against oppression by the mighty; the advocate of toleration who re-admitted Jews to England after more than 350 years of exile.

Scholarly and popular debate continues to rage over this complex and contradictory character. But what is Oliver Cromwell doing in a book about Welsh heroes and villains? This is a man who only visited Wales twice in his life; once with an army to suppress several thousand of its disgruntled inhabitants, and once on a flying visit en route for Ireland and bloody conquest.

Well, Cromwell was by descent a Welshman and showed a close interest in the well-being of the land of his fathers. For this attention, he was hailed as a native hero by some and damned as a foreign tyrant by others. His memory and legacy have been fought over by opposed Welsh interests in the centuries since his death. Although many today see him as 'God's Englishman', Cromwell has also had a peculiar knack of dividing opinion among his ancestral countrymen.

BACKGROUND: OLIVER CROMWELL ALIAS WILLIAMS

Hilary Mantel's Booker-prize-winning novel *Wolf Hall* is a fictionalised study of Henry VIII's chief minister, Thomas Cromwell, and not the place where you would expect to encounter snatches of Welsh conversation. However, in her

1500s Putney, we catch a young and near-vagrant Cromwell exchanging a few phrases of Welsh with his brother-in-law Morgan Williams – an important character in our story.

Williams hailed from Glamorgan, possibly the Whitchurch area, then a hamlet, now a Cardiff suburb. He moved to Putney and married Thomas Cromwell's sister Katherine. Cromwell's star rose until he became the most powerful commoner in England and Wales (and was the man responsible for the Acts of Union which united the two countries in the 1530s and 1540s). It is no surprise then that the Williamses wanted to broadcast their family ties with the great man. Thus Morgan's son Richard adopted a composite surname 'Williams alias Cromwell', and it is from this line that the future Lord Protector was descended.

By the 1600s the family had moved to Huntingdonshire, but did not forget their Welsh heritage. They commissioned family trees reaching back to ancient Welsh princes and filled their windows with heraldic glass showing their Welsh connections. When the future Lord Protector married in 1620, he was described as 'Oliv[er] Cromwell alias Williams', while another document of 1631 presents him as 'Oliver Williams alias Cromwell'. When he wrote in 1647 to the Welsh Archbishop of York, John Williams, Cromwell addressed him as a kinsman. Somewhere within the Cromwellian shell still lay a Williams.

Contemporaries were aware of Oliver's heritage, and some Welshmen attempted to use this to gain patronage or approval. A 1658 book of prophecies by Welshman Thomas Pugh lauded Cromwell as a true Welsh hero, a deliverer of Welsh blood whose coming had been foreseen centuries before. A year previously, a Meirionnydd man had hoped that Cromwell would sponsor his scheme for establishing a national college in Wales, 'he being descended, as they say, from Wales'.

LORD PROTECTOR AND WELSH PRINCE

The symbols of power used by Lord Protector Cromwell were striking in their Welshness. His personal seal combined the heraldry of the ancient princes of Powys, Glamorgan, Ardudwy and Gwent. At his lying-in-state and funeral (organised by a Glamorgan man), the political iconography included the red dragon of Cadwaladr and more of those medieval Welsh kings. When this East Anglian farmer wanted the clout of some noble blood to underpin his authority, he looked to his Welsh forebears.

HERO: THE PURITANS

Wales was staunchly royalist during the civil wars of the 1640s and 1650s. Few there responded positively to Cromwell's Welsh ancestry. However, a select band of Welsh men and women did see him as a native hero in the mould of Pugh's deliverer. These were the Puritans.

These puritans were a diverse group of religious radicals who believed that the Reformation in England and Wales had not gone far enough in purging the church of its corrupted Roman Catholic past. They were the intellectual and spiritual forefathers of the nonconformist denominations which became so influential in Wales during the 19th century. The civil wars were brought about in no small measure because of puritan discontent with the religious policies of Charles I.

The puritans in Wales at this time were a small, scattered and feeble force. With the resistance of the Long Parliament against King Charles, however, Welsh puritans expanded in numbers and influence. A key figure in assisting their cause was Oliver Cromwell.

At the beginning of the Long Parliament, Cromwell was a relatively obscure backbench MP sitting for Cambridge, and certainly not the obvious sponsor of the embattled band of early Welsh puritans. However, perhaps because of his ancestral links with areas in south-east Wales where Welsh puritans were concentrated, in early 1642 he presented a petition to Parliament on behalf of

Pennard Church on the Gower

Monmouthshire puritans who were being harassed by the authorities. Shortly after, he presented the case of puritans in Pennard on the Gower against their minister. Contacts had evidently been forged between the Welsh religious radicals and Cromwell, a man who was beginning to make a name for himself as a militant opponent of Charles I. These religious connections would come to dominate Welsh attitudes towards Cromwell down the centuries.

Cromwell became increasingly involved in Welsh affairs after the Parliamentarians had defeated the Royalists. He became a major Welsh landowner in 1648 as a grateful parliament granted its most successful soldier lands taken from the royalist Earl of Worcester. These included large estates in Monmouthshire and virtually all of the Gower Peninsula. There is some evidence that Cromwell used these lands to support like-minded friends and associates, and to drive forward the puritanisation of a country which many saw as mired in religious ignorance.

A project which was particularly close to Cromwell's heart was the Commission for the Propagation of the Gospel in Wales (1650–3). This was a state-sponsored body which supported radical puritans in their efforts to convert the people of Wales to a more reformed brand of Protestantism.

Cromwell was deeply committed to the commission, and the Long Parliament's refusal to support it in 1653 was the occasion for his dissolving the assembly at the head of a company of soldiers. The Commission had allowed Welsh puritans to spread their message with the backing of the state, and most were deeply grateful to Cromwell for his support. Here was a Welsh hero indeed, working against religious ignorance and apathy in an effort to raise the spiritual condition of their benighted country. A pamphlet from hundreds of Cromwell's Welsh supporters in 1656 praised his 'most Christian and favourable understanding of us ... the poor saints of Wales, who were ... so much your joy'. This was not the only perspective at the time, however.

VILLAIN: ROYALISTS AND ANGLICANS

Welsh royalism had stemmed in no small part from the people's deep attachment to the Church of England, of which the monarch was, and is, the head. Support for parliament in Wales was meagre outside of the small core of Welsh puritans, and royalist defeat left a very bitter taste in the mouths of many. With a narrow support base, the parliamentarian regimes of the 1640s and 1650s faced serious resistance in Wales from the supporters of the old regime: the royalists and Anglicans. This was particularly the case after the deeply unpopular execution of the king and the radical initiative of the Propagation Commission which seemed to strike at much of what these conservatives and moderates held dear.

Bitterness and resentment at the treatment of Anglican Wales found a ready focus in the puritans' principal friend and ally: Cromwell.

This hostility can be found in the poetry of the period which articulates some of the anger and resentment at Cromwell and his Welsh puritan allies. The metaphysical poet Henry Vaughan of Breconshire, for example, wrote bitterly in the 1650s that Wales was living 'in the shadow of death; where destruction passeth for propagation'.

Given the political situation, it was difficult to criticise Cromwell directly, of course, but some suggestive evidence of this anti-Cromwellian sentiment can be found in Welsh-language poetry. Bards like John Griffith and Robert ap Huw spoke of their longing for the old Church of England and their horror at the puritan forces which Cromwell had unleashed. Huw Morys of Llansilin turned to allegory to criticise the regime, describing peace-loving parishioners as *defaid*, sheep, but Cromwell was *Y Llwynog*, The Fox, that preyed upon them.

A majority of the Welsh population at this time would have supported such comments, seeing recent events as a catastrophe and Cromwell as the arch-villain of the piece. The Restoration of monarchy in 1660 allowed such sentiments to be expressed more freely. So we find John Griffith composing a 'Song Made on the Ransacking the Country in the Time of Oliver Cromwell's Protectorship', while Huw Morys left his allegory behind to pass judgement on Cromwell and his fanatical 'traitors' in impassioned poems which likened the Protector to King Herod.

Huw Morys's memorial in Dyffryn Ceiriog

A CONTESTED LEGACY

There was a fierce division of opinion over Oliver Cromwell's legacy in Wales which was largely fought along lines of religious (and thus political) allegiance. The dominant note was sounded by the royalist Anglican clergy who returned to their pulpits in force after the restoration of Charles II.

The religious and political establishments had a vested interest in portraying 'Usurper Cromwell' as a demon who had brought only war, religious chaos and tyrannous rule in 'the late wretched times'. They argued that following his type of nonconformist puritan politics would bring a return to anarchy. They did so, however, partly because the number of nonconformists, 'the spawn of the fanatics in the time of Oliver's usurpation', had expanded worryingly in many parts of Wales as a result of Cromwell's initiatives.

This was not a fleeting backlash against the Lord Protector. For decades Welsh Anglicans peddled the image of Cromwell as a disloyal tyrant who had brought nothing but misery and confusion. The classic 1703 text by churchman Ellis Wynne, *Gweledigaethau Y Bardd Cwsg* ('Visions of the Sleeping Bard'), contained numerous references to Cromwell and his 'murderous Roundheads'.

This was a hot topic in the Glamorgan parish of Coity even in 1790, when Thomas Davies reminded his congregation of the 'havoc and devastation... sacrilege and cruelty... committed throughout the land' when the puritans were in power. He warned darkly, 'the same restless factious spirit lurks still in the dark, and only waits a fit opportunity of breaking out, with redoubled force unto all manner of outrage and rebellion from which, Good Lord, deliver us!'

Welsh nonconformists had a different tale to tell. Yet it was difficult to extol Cromwell's achievements while the Anglican establishment was in control. Cromwell as hero was an underground image preserved by radicals such as the historian Iolo Morganwg. He relied on Baptist works of history that portrayed the religiously tolerant Cromwell in a much more positive light than the uncompromising Charles I. However, the growing strength of religious nonconformity in the rapidly-industrialising

Oliver Cromwell

communities of 19th-century Wales, along with a new emphasis on ideas of liberty and toleration following the French and American revolutions, brought a new and heroic Cromwell before the Welsh public.

Research by Dr Marion Löffler has begun to reveal how Cromwell was transformed into a kind of national hero in Welsh and English-language newspapers, books and journals. His Welsh ancestry was rediscovered and proclaimed in many works, even in a Tory newspaper like *The Western Mail*! For the new populations of industrial Wales, here was a hero who was one of their own. Moreover, he was a torchbearer for their interests – *'Gwroniad Rhyddid'* ('A Hero of Liberty'), a founder of democracy and, most importantly, a man who had helped and cherished the spiritual ancestors of 19th-century nonconformists: the puritans.

Statues were erected in front of chapels; the new urban centres acquired 'Cromwell Streets'; *eisteddfodau* were presented with poetry and learned treatises on Cromwell and his times. He had become 'Olifer Cromwel', a *Cymro* imbued with what were believed to be Welsh national traits, such as 'his devout feelings towards his religion, his impetuous and fiery temper, his daring and fearless spirit', and a love of light, liberty and democracy.

TWO CROMWELLS

In 1866 a young Llandeilo painter, Oliver Owen, was committed to two years hard labour for bigamy. One of the aliases he had given in his double life was 'Oliver Cromwell'. His choice of alternative identity may have been ironic, but it is suggestive of the growth in the public awareness of Cromwell in Wales during this period.

A less hysterical version of the positive Victorian image has endured in the popular imagination, although few today are aware of the Welsh ancestry which so fired 19th-century commentators. Increasing secularisation and a decline in religious observance have cut off the well spring for much of the enthusiasm and interest in Cromwell. There is residual support in Wales for his anti-authoritarian image and championing of liberty, but the decline of the radical Left has further diluted these impulses. The labels of commitment, of Cromwell as 'hero' or 'villain', belong to an earlier time of inter-religious conflict.

There is no question that Cromwell had a constructive programme for the Welsh, 'the poor people of God' as he called them. Through initiatives like the Propagation Commission, he thought he could help bring them into the light of a new spiritual awakening. In part he succeeded, helping foster nonconformist communities in Wales which would one day hail him as a far-sighted deliverer of his native people – a latter-day Moses. There was a significant cost, however. His legacy was an ambiguous one and a fundamental religious and political divide appeared in Wales after the Civil War. Nonconformists and their political heirs, the Whigs, Liberals, Labour, saw Cromwell as a hero. But there was an alternative vision which was popular down to the 19th century. In this view Cromwell was not simply a villain, but no less than the devil incarnate.

Further reading:
Ian Gentles, *Oliver Cromwell: God's Warrior and the English Revolution* (2011)

8

DISEASE: THE UNSEEN VILLAIN IN WELSH HISTORY

Alun Withey

Throughout history, epidemic diseases have preyed upon our ancestors, weeding out not only the elderly, weak and vulnerable but the healthy and vigorous. Despite the relative success of modern medicine in treating many conditions which were previously fatal, the threat of epidemics and pandemics – most recently Swine Flu – continues to haunt us, stirring up popular fear and collective memories of past outbreaks. So despite the passage of more than three centuries, for example, we can still relate to the fear of the famous diarist Samuel Pepys as he walked around the streets of plague-ridden London in 1665, noticing the many doors painted with red crosses, and 'God Have Mercy' written ominously upon them.

But how have Wales and Welsh people fared in this story of sickness? Was Wales a hotbed of epidemic diseases? Actually, historians haven't so far paid much attention to the subject, but the evidence is interesting. Certainly Welsh people have suffered through the centuries, as we'll see. But occasionally, Wales, its landscape and geography, have also served to protect its people from the worst effects of plague and pestilence.

PLAGUES AND POXES

The first recorded epidemic in Wales occurred in the sixth century. In AD526, Saint Brioc of Brittany came to Ceredigion and wrote that the whole region was 'overwhelmed by a great catastrophe'. This was *Y vad velen* ('the yellow plague'), part of an epidemic outbreak noted across Britain. Outbreaks of a plague-like disease recurred in 526 and 537, but a further epidemic of *Y vad velen* in 547 caught the imagination of Welsh poets for the next several hundred years.

The biographer of Saint Teilo vividly described it as coming over the land like the 'column of a watery cloud'. It was this 'yellow pestilence' which 'seized Maelgwyn, king of North Wales, and destroyed his country'. According to legend, Maelgwyn sought sanctuary in the church of Llanrhos but was restless. Unable to resist looking out upon his kingdom, he peeped through the keyhole of the church door, but even this tiny exposure to the outside air was enough for him to catch the infection. Curiosity, in this case, killed the king.

Throughout the medieval period, a succession of plagues and sicknesses continued to haunt Wales, but references are scant. Various medieval Welsh annals and chronicles refer fleetingly to extreme events such as epidemics or natural phenomena which occurred from time to time. In 896, it was even recorded that a plague of vermin 'like moles' fell from the skies and devoured everything they encountered! But the fear of sickness was certainly deeply entrenched in Welsh culture as it was elsewhere, and it was common for diaries and letters to contain references to troubling 'new' diseases. In 1657, the Flintshire puritan Philip Henry made reference to reports of 'fourscore children sickened of a new disease' in 'Swansey in Glamorganshire'. In 1734, the Welsh MP John Campbell wrote from London to his young son, Prys, worrying about an outbreak of 'violent coughs' affecting children 'all about the countrey'.

Some diseases, however, were so abhorrent that they even entered popular culture. Few achieved the same levels of infamy as did *Y Frech Wen* – the smallpox. Smallpox was a virulent disease which became epidemic in 17th- and 18th-century Britain, and accounted for around 15% of total deaths in the period. Wales certainly did not escape. In 1722–3, 71 people died of the disease in Carmarthen, and further severe outbreaks followed over the next few years.

What made smallpox seem all the more vicious was that it was most often a disease of childhood. Surviving it was almost a rite of passage for children, but there was a sting in the tail since recovery (though it gave immunity from further infection) often left the sufferer horribly scarred. Smallpox also came with a certain degree of social stigma, leaving scarred survivors ostracised from their friends and families. It could run rampant through families and communities and, in the days before inoculation, there was little defence. So feared was it that advertisements for servants in 18th-century households sometimes stipulated that applicants must already have had the disease, to prevent them bringing the infection into a family.

The disfiguring nature of smallpox found its way into literature and poetry.

The medieval Welsh poet Tudur Aled wrote of the visible effects of smallpox, describing warrior's shields as being dented and pitted as though with smallpox. Another, Cadwaladr Roberts of Pennant Melangell, bemoaned the ravages of the 'pox of pain' upon his own face in the 1730s. No longer attractive to a 'beautiful and unstained girl' Cadwaladr believed that only a 'keen witch' would now wed him, 'this grubby elf with perforated skin'. But even apparently innocent verse, such as children's nursery rhymes, sometimes carried more sinister undertones. The Welsh nursery rhyme 'Cân nant yr eira' tells of a small boy who wears his beaverskin hat low upon his brow to hide his smallpox scars and dimples. Something of this disease still echoes in modern times. In 1962, smallpox hit the town of Maerdy in Rhondda. Sufferers were warned by doctors that they could expect different treatment by friends and neighbours; the stigma of smallpox scars, it seems, was not consigned to the past.

Epidemics of gastro-enteric diseases, such as dysentery, were also common in the 17th and 18th centuries. Dysentery, known by contemporaries as The Bloody Flux, was a disease spread by infected food and water, and also by flies. This was a summer disease, more virulent in warm and humid weather, and was especially common in coastal towns and especially ports, introduced by visiting ships whose crew carried the infection. It was common in reports of epidemics for writers to include shocking vignettes of the aftermath, such as grass growing over the streets and not enough people being left to bury the dead. Just such a report was included in a letter relating an outbreak of the disease in Cardiff in 1697.

Perhaps most infamous of all epidemic diseases is bubonic plague. How badly affected was Wales by this most dreaded infection? Bubonic plague was present in England from the Middle Ages until the middle of the 17th century although it tended to be a visitor rather than a permanent resident. It moved rapidly through densely populated areas which meant that it was more often a disease of the towns although rural parishes were certainly affected. Influenced by weather patterns, it tended to peak in the late summer months and affected adolescents and adults, more than children, and both sexes alike. Wales certainly suffered a number of outbreaks, and larger towns, and port towns in particular, were badly hit. Carmarthen suffered five major outbreaks, in 1604, 1606, 1611, 1651 and 1657.

IN PRESTEIGNE HEALTH

Presteigne suffered four outbreaks of plague, its authorities threatening to restrict people's movements in 1636 to prevent them spreading the disease. That same year, one unscrupulous man from a neighbouring parish was actually bound over by magistrates for threatening to go to Presteigne to deliberately contract the plague so that he could infect his estranged wife!

Other towns, such as Wrexham and Haverfordwest were also particularly badly hit while, at the peak of an outbreak in Chester in 1603, over 150 people were dying every week. An outbreak of plague in Tenby in 1650 is supposed to have killed 500 people when the town had a population of less than a thousand. This occurred at a time of economic hardship in the town, through declining trade and fishing revenues. It was reported that the mayor had to employ people to retrieve food from outside the boundaries, as nobody would dare to enter the pestiferous town. Neither was it only towns that were hit. The isolated outbreak of plague which hit Bedwellty parish in Monmouthshire killed 82 people in 1638, the parish registers revealing a solemn tale of mortality. The diarist Walter Powell in fact wrote that the disease was 'very hot in diverse parts of Monmouthshire'.

But how did Wales fare in comparison to the rest of Britain? Actually, although the rates of plague mortality here are chilling, it does seem that Wales suffered less than other parts of Britain. Why could this have been? One explanation is that of the actual landscape of Wales itself. Bubonic plague was less virulent at higher altitudes and in colder environments, both of which abound in Wales. There were fewer large towns in Wales than in other areas, while many parts of the Welsh countryside were relatively sparsely populated, making it more difficult for the disease to establish itself. The exception to this was Wales's coastline. With well over a hundred miles of coast, and numerous large and small ports, there was ample opportunity for the introduction of disease and it is probably no coincidence that port towns, and also towns along rivers and trading routes, were the worst hit.

DISEASE IN INDUSTRIAL WALES

Living conditions certainly did not do anything to check the spread of disease. In pre-industrial Wales, housing and diet were both proverbially poor. Welsh rural cottages (uncharitably referred to by one English observer as resembling 'great blots of cow turd' on the landscape) were often basic at best, and squalid at worst. Close proximity to animals meant contact with dung and flies, and clay floors covered with straw trapped filth and soaked up urine. Since people did not routinely wash themselves, infestations of lice and skin conditions were common. Things were little better in Welsh towns, the poor dwelling in small alleys and courtyards away from their more affluent neighbours.

The practice of emptying human waste onto the street left many public spaces as little more than open sewers. Even as late as 1740, the authorities in Aberystwyth chastised townspeople for 'lay(ing) downe their dunghill opposite their doors'. Visitors to towns from rural areas risked infection through encountering diseases from which they had no immunity. From two or three centuries' distance, it is perhaps difficult for us now to imagine that such conditions existed on our own doorsteps.

As Wales began to industrialise, patterns of mortality also began to change. In the 19th century, ever-growing numbers of migrant workers poured into newly created industrial towns from both within and outside Wales. The need to accommodate workers quickly necessitated the rapid building of large numbers of houses, often quickly erected and with few rooms and little living space. It was not unusual for several families to occupy one house, and the proximity of large numbers of people, and in sometimes squalid conditions, allowed diseases to spread with alarming speed.

George Childs's watercolour of Dowlais Ironworks, 1840

Even the industrial environment itself brought new dangers. The new powerhouses of production, such as the iron works at Penydarren and Dowlais, pumped sulphurous chemicals into the air, while the thick coal dust of the pits clogged up the lungs of generations of Welsh miners. One of the worst offenders was the newly-developing Swansea copper industry. The smoke from copper manufacture was brimming with dangerous and harmful by-products, including sulphuric acid and even arsenic. Daily exposure to this toxic fug could exacerbate a range of bronchial conditions, and also lower immunity, serving to increase incidences of other diseases such as consumption and fever.

A LUNGFUL A DAY KEEPS THE DOCTOR AWAY...

Copper masters fought back and argued that not only was copper smoke harmless, it was actually healthy! A report to the Board of Health by the Swansea doctor Thomas Williams in 1854, asserted that the presence of copper smoke was in fact extremely beneficial since its antiseptic properties acted as a protective cordon to keep disease at bay.

Cholera and typhus were indicative of the sorts of epidemic diseases to torment industrial Welsh towns. Cholera, caused through contaminated drinking water, caused vomiting, diarrhoea and cramps which, in severe cases, could cause death within a matter of hours. Typhus and typhoid claimed many lives across Wales between the 1830s and 1860s, and often hit the poor hardest, not least as they often swept through institutions such as workhouses with alarming speed and ferocity.

Cholera cemetery, Tredegar

In the mid 19th-century, Merthyr parish included prospering towns such as Aberdare, then an iron-producing town of around 45,000 inhabitants. In 1849 the parish was visited by an outbreak of cholera killing more than 1500 people. In the 1854 Public Health Act enquiry into the outbreak, a local doctor, David Davies, reported on the lack of drainage and clean water serving Aberdare, noting that inhabitants still emptied their waste out of upstairs windows onto the open street. Davies was a key figure in the provision of clean water for the town through the construction of a new reservoir, and also established a fever hospital there in 1871, one of many such institutions beginning to appear around Wales during this period.

But if the 19th century is often viewed as the harbinger of 'modern' or 'scientific' medicine, it is certainly not true that new developments were always welcomed with open arms. Vaccination was a hot topic in 19th-century Wales. The introduction of inoculations for smallpox, cowpox and measles was adopted swiftly in many areas, and in fact was embedded in law in 1853, making it mandatory to inoculate infants.

Measles was another major killer in industrial Wales. In Blaenafon in 1870, a measles outbreak increased the mortality rate from 22 to 166 per 1000 births and, at its height, six or seven children were dying there every day. But there was also something of a backlash. In Newport, some parents argued against the safety of the vaccinations, and were in fact prosecuted for refusing to present their children according to the requirements of the Vaccination Acts. On July 31, 1869, the *Western Mail* reported on a conference about vaccination held in Cardiff, where a certain Dr Haviland reported his disgust at seeing children forcefully injected even in the waiting rooms of railway stations by overzealous overseers. The case for the success of vaccination, he argued, was unproven.

VILLAINS... AND HEROES?

We could simply stop there and conclude that the people of Wales, throughout history, have been bedevilled by all manner of epidemic and endemic diseases attacking minds and bodies and leaving chilling traces in the records of our ancestors. But, in the midst of all this villainy, it is perhaps nicer to reflect on one particular hero to whom Wales can legitimately lay claim.

On July 5, 1948, after much brokering, negotiation and even a dramatic stand-off with the British Medical Association, the then Secretary of State for Health launched the new National Health Service in a weary, post-war Britain. For the first time, health care was available to the whole of the UK population free of charge, effectively ending a tiered system of medical provision, and opening up a range of treatment options to those previously unable to afford, or reliant on charity. Despite contemporary criticisms of the NHS, it still provides millions of people in Wales and beyond with a level of healthcare which, only a few generations ago, would have seemed Utopian. And who was this social-minded minister? Aneurin Bevan of Tredegar.

Further reading:
Alun Withey, *Physick and the Family: Health, medicine and care in Wales, 1600– 1750* (2011)

Aneurin Bevan addresses the masses

9

THE COPPER KINGS: INDUSTRIALISTS AS DESPOILERS AND IMPROVERS

H.V. Bowen

Entrepreneurs have not had a good press in Welsh history. The coal owners, iron masters and steel barons who drove the process of rapid and often brutal industrialisation have often been characterised as exploiters, despoilers, and oppressors. They made their fortunes by inflicting misery and poverty on a downtrodden population who toiled away for meagre reward in mines, forges, and smelting works. What is more, these capitalist parasites have regularly been depicted as aliens – above all as English intruders – who came to Wales in search of profits and then retreated to their country estates to count their loot, leaving behind a ravaged landscape and a shattered people.

Of course, such crude descriptions are the stuff of caricature, but they have had a long life. They continue to colour views of the past to a surprising degree, and this means that the Welsh people can still be characterised as 'victims' who fell foul of some of the most ruthless 'villains' in our history. Indeed, not so very long ago, the (rightly) celebrated socialist historian Gwyn Alf Williams wrote in characteristically colourful fashion that into Wales came 'the intrusive and massively endowed entrepreneurs from England, Anthony Bacon, Crawshays, Guests, Homfrays, Wilkinsons, collaring a world market.' And, he went on, 'They exploited all the resources and all the people they could get hold of with [an] … irresponsible and single-minded fervour.' As far as Williams was concerned, the charge sheet against these men was very long indeed, and all they cared about was the bottom line.

Colourful and celebrated historian, Gwyn Alf Williams

Recent detailed research is now beginning to revise this picture. In particular, in *Hope and Heartbreak* Russell Davies has pointed out, and illustrated with many examples, that the Welsh were not passive as industrialisation reshaped the economies and societies of both North and South Wales after 1700. He notes that 'The Welsh proved themselves to be remarkably capable of establishing capitalist enterprises; they were adept at taking their opportunities.' And he observes that 'The Welsh also revealed themselves to be inventive and adaptive people.'

Why, then, has it taken us so long to recognise this? Certainly both the socialist and nationalist traditions of Welsh history writing have focused on the negative aspects of the unregulated and often deeply damaging capitalism that began to sweep over large parts of Wales during the late 18th century.

But also it is perhaps the case that the general social and religious milieu in Wales over the last three hundred years or so has meant that Welsh people have always been somewhat suspicious of those who have worshipped at the feet of Mammon. As a result, entrepreneurs and the makers of money have often been treated with thinly veiled contempt and no little hostility, even though they have been key agents of 'improvement', 'progress', and economic development.

ENTREPRENEURS AS HEROES (BUT NOT IN WALES)

Such attitudes towards the Captains of Industry can of course be found in other parts of Britain. But it is quite striking that historians of the 'British' Industrial Revolution are much more inclined than historians of Wales to highlight and praise the efforts of the entrepreneurs whose collective endeavours transformed Britain into the 'workshop of the world' by 1850.

There are many factors – both general and specific – that combine to explain the early development of Britain's industrialised economy. But sensible historians still pay careful attention to human agency or the actions of key individuals. Thus, in what are described as 'heroic accounts' of the Industrial Revolution, inventors, manufacturers, and entrepreneurs are identified as the prime movers in the complex processes that transformed Britain.

These heroes cast a long shadow over the history books but only very rarely is there a mention of any Welshman or entrepreneur who was at work at Wales. This is despite the fact that, according to UN criteria, Wales was the world's first industrial nation by 1851. Indeed, the historians of British industrialisation persist in placing the Welsh economy at the very outer edges of the story. As a result, the history of the Industrial Revolution remains a history of a very English revolution.

FROM COKE TO MULE

A list of British industrial heroes includes practical improvers such as Abraham Darby who used coke to smelt iron at Coalbrookdale in 1709; Thomas Newcomen who in 1712 improved the first steam engine developed by Thomas Savery; and Henry Cort who in 1783–4 used his 'puddling' process for refining pig iron in order to produce bar iron. Also included are the inventors of the flying shuttle (John Kay); spinning jenny (James Hargreaves); water frame (Richard Arkwright); and 'mule' (Samuel Crompton). And then there are the great entrepreneurs such as Josiah Wedgwood; Matthew Boulton; and various members of the Crowley family.

WHEN COPPEROPOLIS RULED THE WORLD

The absence of Wales from textbook histories of the Industrial Revolution is explained in large part by the stubbornly Anglocentric outlook of most of the authors. But the omission is nonetheless puzzling because Wales provides abundant examples of innovation and enterprise that were 'world-leading' in their day.

Parys Mountain, Anglesey, where enormous copper seams were opened up in the 18th century

The remains of the Llansamlet copper and arsenic works in the 1950s

No example is better than that provided by the entrepreneurial endeavours underpinning the dramatic growth of the copper industry centred in the Swansea and Neath valleys, and then later around Llanelli. By any standards what the copper kings achieved was remarkable and should place them in the very first rank of British entrepreneurs.

There is of course no copper ore to be found near Swansea, and the reason that the copper industry developed in the region is because it possessed good river navigation and, above all, abundant local supplies of coal. During the 18th century around twenty tons of coal was required to produce one ton of unrefined copper, so it was much more efficient and cost-effective to carry copper ore to Swansea than it was to ship out large quantities of coal in order to smelt the ore at source. Through trial and error, what became known as the 'Welsh' or 'Swansea' method of copper smelting was developed. This involved successive 'roastings' of copper ore in a series of reverbatory furnaces set up in smelting 'houses', which in the early days were in fact little more than cottages.

At first, during the early 18th century, it was primarily ore from Ireland and Cornwall that found its way into the smelting houses of south-west Wales.

Then, after 1770, enormous seams were opened up on Parys Mountain and supplies from Anglesey came to the fore. But the voracious appetite of the smelters soon depleted the British copper mines, and in order to sustain the industry the net had to be cast much further afield.

In what was a quite remarkable development, from the 1820s the Swansea entrepreneurs sought out new sources of ore in the wider world, and they turned their attention to Cuba, Chile, South Australia, North America and elsewhere. They set up extended transoceanic supply chains in order to bring large quantities of ore to the river Tawe, and the copper barques known as 'Cape Horners' came to symbolise Swansea's growing maritime presence in the wider world.

Far-distant parts of the world were yoked to the economy of the lower Swansea valley. Places such as the port of Valparaiso in Chile and Burra in Australia became 'suburbs' of Swansea. The El Cobre mines in eastern Cuba were revived and expanded by Welsh copper companies, with a large slave-labour force working in appalling conditions to meet the powerful demand of the Swansea smelters.

The effect was to create the world's first globally integrated heavy industry. Into Swansea came ore from multiple overseas sources. The ore was then smelted and fashioned into bars, ingots, bolts, plates, sheets and some manufactured items. The copper, together with some brass, was then exported to markets in Africa, Asia, Europe, North America and elsewhere.

At times during the 19th century the dozen or so copperworks of the lower Swansea valley produced over half of the world's output of smelted copper. Swansea itself became popularly known as 'Copperopolis'. But while this title was in some ways appropriate, it did scant justice to the diversity and sheer intensity of the industrial activity taking place around Swansea. Alongside the copper works were to be found enterprises that specialised in other non-ferrous metals: lead, silver, zinc, tin. Swansea was a hotbed of innovation, a place where science, enterprise, and industry co-mingled. And, as if to acknowledge this, during the mid-19th century Swansea earned the title 'intelligent town' (a description that is as appropriate today as it was then!).

THE COPPER KINGS

So who were the men who spotted the opportunities offered by Swansea and then exploited them with such dramatic effect? Well, as was later the case with industries in other parts of Wales, there were plenty of incomers from over the border, in this case notably from Bristol and London.

Leading the way in 1717 was Dr John Lane, a Bristolian, who moved his works from Neath Abbey and set up a smelter at Landore in what became known as the Llangyfelach works. These works were soon taken on by a partnership involving the London merchant Richard Lockwood, whose connection enabled him to secure a contract to supply Swansea copper to the East India Company.

In 1737, the White Rock works was established by a Bristol Company, whose members included John Coster. This established a connection between the Swansea copper industry and the burgeoning Atlantic slave trade, in which copper rods and 'manillas' were used as trade tokens.

During the second half of the 18th century, incoming investors included the wealthy, restless, London businessman Chauncey Townsend, who founded, among many other enterprises, the Middle Bank works. He was joined in the gathering copper rush by men such as John Freeman, George Pengree, Alexander Raby, Joseph Rotton, and others. Late arrivers from Cornwall included some of the families whose names were to be deeply inscribed into the industrial history and townscape of Swansea: the Vivians who founded the Hafod works in 1810; and the Grenfells who took over several works during the 19th century.

But it would be quite wrong to think that this was an industrial region created and developed solely by Englishmen. Throughout, the skilled labour force was defined by its Welshness, but Welsh entrepreneurs also played their parts in decisive ways.

The Mackworths had long-established industrial concerns in Neath, and the records reveal them to have been manufacturing copper items for sale in India during the 1780s. And, of course, astute incoming investors recognised the need to work with local men who possessed expert knowledge. In this sense the partnership created in 1727 between Swansea-based Robert Morris and London-based Richard Lockwood was one of the most important and enduring. Morris was the man-on-the-spot who knew how the industry worked. Lockwood was the visionary man-of-the-world who understood the importance of demand emanating from markets in The Levant, India, and elsewhere. As a result, Morris, Lockwood & Co. blazed a trail for others to follow, and the firm survived until 1793.

Above all, though, stood Thomas Williams, who during the 1780s and 1790s completely dominated the British copper industry. Although not a local man, the solicitor from Anglesey was extraordinarily adept at making things happen and bringing people and processes together. Williams was not an inventor and did not leave us with any designs, gadgets, or engines, but he was perhaps the greatest entrepreneur ever produced by Wales. Yet, although well known in Wales, he has largely escaped the notice of English historians as well as the author of a recent history of Welsh entrepreneurs. Today Williams would probably be described as 'multi-tasking facilitator' or something similar. What he did during the late 18th century was organise and integrate the Welsh copper industry into a single joined-up enterprise. He cornered the market in ore, not just by exploiting the rich resources of Parys Mountain but also by undercutting the powerful lobby of Cornish copper mine-owners. At every opportunity he ran rings round powerful rivals such as John Vivian and Matthew Boulton, the great manufacturing impresario from Birmingham. Williams's Parys Mine Company took over the Upper Bank works in Swansea in 1782, and secured an exclusive contract to supply copper to the East India Company. He built ships to carry ore from Amlwch to Swansea, and his vessels then took smelted copper on to London. In short, he showed how an essentially local industry could be organised to become a global industry; and others built on his legacy during the boom years of the 19th century.

THE BALANCE SHEET

Without doubt the copper kings deserve much credit for what they achieved. They were trailblazers in taking the products of the Industrial Revolution into the wider world; and they put Swansea at the heart of a global network. And they did more. They enjoyed their wealth and lavished much of it on houses, parks, and gardens, such as those to be found at Singleton and Clyne. But they did not ignore their local responsibilities. They built housing for their workers, provided schools, and funded the construction of chapels and churches. As a result, their influence on the urban environment was profound and long-lasting.

Scratch beneath the surface of Swansea today and everywhere you will find it engrained with copper: in Morriston (Morris Town); Hafod (Trevivian); and Pentrechwyth (Grenfell Town); in the leafier parts of west Swansea; and of course in the valley itself. But all this 'progress' came at a terrible price, because the local landscape, and especially the formerly beautiful Tawe valley was completely devastated by the process of industrialisation that went into slow decline from 1890 onwards. The smelters poisoned people, plants, and animals, and when they walked away from their works they left behind the largest derelict industrial landscape in Western Europe. They created a stunning, unforgettable, physical monument to the very worst excesses of industrial capitalism.

By the 1960s the people of the lower Swansea valley were living in what was routinely described as a 'moonscape'. It was an environment that was treeless and grassless, peppered with giant slag heaps and industrial ruins. Only the heroic efforts of those involved with the Lower Swansea Valley Project, established exactly fifty years ago, served to bring the valley back to life and make it once more a place that is fit for people to live and work in. The valley is now green again, and indeed it is now sometimes hard to believe that it was once one of the most important crucibles of Britain's Industrial Revolution.

Further reading:
www.welshcopper.org.uk

10

SIR THOMAS PICTON: HERO OF WATERLOO AND 'BLOOD-SOAKED GOVERNOR' OF TRINIDAD

Chris Evans

Sir Thomas Picton is a Welsh hero. It's official. The Edwardian city hall in Cardiff is home to a set of twelve marble statues, the 'Heroes of Wales', and Picton is one of them. He is an improbable companion to Saint David and a set of obscure medieval princes.

His is not a name with much resonance today, but a century ago things were different. Thomas Picton earned his fame soldiering in Spain; he was one of Wellington's celebrated Peninsular generals. In 1815, when Napoleon made his escape from Elba, Pembrokeshire-born Picton was once again with Wellington, this time at Waterloo. Sir Thomas Picton

Picton led the 'Fighting 3rd' from the front, as ever, and paid the price: he was the most senior British officer to die at Waterloo. As such, his posthumous reputation was high. Colonial frontier towns in Canada, Australia and New Zealand were named in his honour, and he remains the only Welshman buried in St Paul's Cathedral, where his memorial stands close to Wellington's own tomb.

PICTON MEMORIALS

Aside from the statue in the 'Heroes of Wales' gallery in Cardiff City Hall, there are two eye-catching memorials to Sir Thomas Picton. One is in Carmarthen. It is an imposing stone obelisk erected in 1847 to replace a still larger monument, modelled on Trajan's Column in Rome, which had been erected twenty years earlier. (This earlier memorial had not been equal to the Welsh weather and soon fell into disrepair.) The second major memorial is in St Paul's Cathedral. Visitors will find Picton's tomb in the north transept. It is topped by a bust portraying the Welshman as a Roman general.

I found him a rough, foul-
mouthed devil as ever lived, but
no man could do better...

The Duke of Wellington's
judgement on Picton

If, in afterlife, Picton acquired the aura of a Victorian hero, his own life fell short of the chivalrous ideals the Victorians admired. His unflinching courage was beyond question but in other respects he was lacking. He was a roisterer, a duellist, a fornicator and, as his old commander noted, possessed of a famously abusive tongue. These defects were not unique to Picton, but there was also a singular stain on his character, one that stemmed from his years as military governor of Trinidad. Picton's regime (1797–1803) was brutally authoritarian, so much so that he was recalled to London to stand trial for his excesses.

Trinidad is the most southerly of the Caribbean islands, lying just off the coast of Venezuela. The island was claimed for Spain by Columbus in 1498 and it remained part of the Spanish empire until it was seized by the British in 1797. Trinidad had remained an out-of-the-way, neglected place in the three centuries of Spanish rule, but once it fell under British control, change came rapidly. This was an age of upheaval in the West Indies, where a huge slave insurrection had brought down the French colonial regime in Saint-Domingue (modern Haiti). The implosion of Saint-Domingue, which had supplied nearly half the world's sugar before the slave rising in 1791, sent sugar prices soaring and planters off in search of available land. Trinidad, where there was plenty of undisturbed soil, suddenly became the new frontier of the Caribbean sugar sector.

Investment surged into Trinidad and so, inevitably it seemed, did slaves. Slaves had been present in the Spanish era, but they had seeped in, fewer than one hundred annually; in the first ten years of British occupation nearly 23,000 were landed. This was enough to make the future of Trinidad a political issue in Britain. Was the island to be transformed into a grid of slave-worked sugar plantations? The adventurers and eager investors who gravitated to the island in the wake of the British invasion hoped so. Abolitionists in Britain were determined to prevent it. To open up Trinidad's uncultivated interior would mean a vast extension of the slave trade. One abolitionist MP estimated the number of fresh Africans needed to bring Trinidad to the same level of development as Jamaica at *one million*.

Let a portion of that rich and
unopened soil, be sold at a
low price, or granted freely,
to all who will undertake, as
the condition of the tenure...
to settle and cultivate it by the
labor of FREE NEGROES.

An abolitionist proposal
for the pioneering of Trinidad

The abolitionists proposed an alternative. Trinidad should be a laboratory in which forms of tropical agriculture that did not depend upon slave labour should be pioneered.

Trinidad under Picton's rule was no longer an out-of-the-way place. It was at the centre of debates over the future of the British empire.

A mural depicting the death of Picton at Waterloo

Picton had served in the invasion of 1797 and when the bulk of British forces moved on he stayed as Trinidad's military commandant. The island's potential as a slave-worked sugar island was plain enough. Indeed, Governor Picton bought up real estate himself and the slaves to work it. (When emancipation came to the British Caribbean in the 1830s the governor's heir, Revd Thomas Picton of Iscoed, was compensated for the 98 slaves held captive on the Aranjuez plantation.) The building of a plantation order had pre-conditions though. One was unremitting discipline. In this, Trinidad was deficient; it had long been a haven for runaways, deserters and desperadoes. Under Picton that was to change. He set about dispensing a brand of justice that was seldom tempered by mercy. The island's population was cowed by a wave of exemplary executions. As for the growing numbers of forced African labourers, they were subjected to a slave code of Picton's own design. Delinquents who were sent for immediate execution might consider themselves lucky; others had to endure mutilation and torture.

Iscoed, the shell of a fine Georgian mansion, is all that remains of Picton's 800-acre estate overlooking the Tywi estuary

Thomas Picton's new regime was vicious but it brought striking results. Sugar exports totalled 8.4 million lbs in 1799; by 1802 they were 14.2 million lbs. The price of slaves, always a good index of a plantation zone's buoyancy, shot upwards. Picton was in high feather. He had been equipped with powers that were little short of dictatorial and he had put them to good use. Stability had been brought to the island and the lassitude of former days had been replaced by vigour and economic growth.

In London, however, it was the abolitionists who were gaining ground. Picton had presided over an economic boom, it had to be conceded, but his methods were not likely to produce stability. They were, the government concluded, unsafe. In 1802 Picton was informed that the administration of Trinidad was to be put on a new footing. Instead of exercising sole authority, he was henceforth to be one of three commissioners: one military (Picton himself), one naval and one civil. The civil commissioner was to have seniority. Picton was not ready to share power with anyone, least of all a civilian. He resigned within a month and sailed for home. Unfortunately for the ex-governor, lurid stories of his iron-fist regime followed him. Before long the stories had hardened into formal charges; they included accusations of torture, false imprisonment and execution without trial. Thomas Picton would have to answer these charges before the Court of King's Bench.

A GENERAL BRED AMONG THE GOATS

The Picton trial was one of the greatest scandals of the age, one that divided the public into pro- and anti-Picton camps. Picton's camp hailed the former governor as an honourable British officer whose no-nonsense approach had been absolutely necessary. Opponents denounced Picton as a tropical tyrant, who had ridden roughshod over the constitutional safeguards to which British subjects were entitled. Picton, it was sneered, 'bred among the goats on the mountains of *Wales*', was incapable of appreciating the 'immortal fabric' of the 'constitution of *England*'.

When the matter came to trial in February 1806, attention was focused on one issue above all others: the torture of a young mulatto, Louisa Calderón, once the concubine of Pedro Ruiz, a rich merchant in Port of Spain. It was alleged that Calderón had colluded with another lover to rob Ruiz. The facts of the robbery were not disputed; all that was lacking in the view of the Spanish magistrate was the confession of Calderón. This she stubbornly refused to make. Governor Picton was therefore asked to authorise the judicial torture of the accused. This was permissible under Spanish law, and Picton had been instructed to apply Spanish law when he had been left in charge of the island back in 1797. Accordingly, he signed the order allowing the investigating magistrate to 'apply the question'. The method of questioning was as follows. Louisa Calderón was suspended from a pulley set in the roof of the torture cell, trussed up so that only one of her legs could dangle freely. She was then lowered onto a sharpened spike set in the floor, her naked foot first, until her entire body weight rested on the spike. This was picketing.

Picketing was not the worst that Port of Spain's gaol had to offer, but it exercised a gruesome fascination for the British public. Prints purporting to illustrate Louisa Calderón's ordeal were in wide circulation. She was shown as a delicately featured damsel, menaced by leering guards. The frisson of horror that the episode aroused in court reflected the youth and sex of the victim. Calderón's age was never definitely settled, but she was certainly young: at the time of her picketing she was not long past puberty. The prosecution made much of her graceful femininity. Her entrance, in a demure white dress and a matching turban, was artfully choreographed. The contrast with Picton, who could never shake off his ruffian air, was unmistakable. The general's protest that she was 'a common Mulatto prostitute, of the vilest class and most corrupt morals', could not dislodge the impression of injured innocence that the prosecution had contrived. (Picton's outrage was more than a little synthetic: his own household in Trinidad had been presided over by a mulatto mistress who bore him four children.) Once the prosecution had satisfied the jury (quite incorrectly) that judicial torture was not sanctioned under Spanish law, the Welsh soldier's fate was sealed. The jurors returned a guilty verdict.

There was more at stake in the trial of Thomas Picton than his individual wrongdoing. The prosecution brought against him shone a light upon some of the most unpalatable aspects of British colonial rule in the Caribbean. The torture inflicted upon Louisa Calderón could not match the atrocities visited upon Picton's slave victims, those who were burned alive or dismembered, but Calderón's sufferings were those of a young woman who was light-skinned and free. They were politically sensational. Unwisely, Picton's lawyers chose to contrast the supposed mildness of Calderón's treatment with the limitless agony to which slave prisoners were subject. They succeeded only in bringing the British public face-to-face with the shocking cruelty that was endemic across the Caribbean. By doing so, they extended the debate beyond the matter of Picton's individual villainy on the island of Trinidad; uncomfortable questions were posed about the validity of slave regimes in general.

Abolitionists had been chipping away at the slave trade bit by bit in the first years of the 19th century. After years of defeat at the hands of a well-organised West Indian lobby, the abolitionists had come to realise that denouncing the slave trade as immoral would get them only so far. Portraying slavery as contrary to the national interest in a time of war was more effective. In this respect, events in Trinidad were grist to their mill. The unfettered expansion of slave agriculture, as practised by Governor Picton, would surely be destabilising. Had not events in Saint-Domingue demonstrated that the mass importation of Africans was as likely to lead to slave revolution as it was to plantation prosperity? Curbing the slave trade was not just an act of humanity; it was a policy of self-preservation. 'I earnestly request', one abolitionist insisted when arguing against flooding Trinidad with slaves, 'it may be observed that my arguments have been addressed, not to the *conscience* of a British Statesman, but to his *prudence* alone.' Picton's trial dramatised the issues in the most vivid way and contributed to the political ascendancy of abolitionism. Within a year of the verdict against Picton in 1806, the Act that abolished Britain's slave trade for ever was passed by Parliament.

Picton's disgrace did not last long. His lawyers secured a retrial in June 1808 at which the legality of torture under Spanish law was established. This led the jury to return a verdict that recognised Picton's behaviour as legal though deplorable. It was exoneration enough. Picton resumed his military career and did so with great success.

Spain was his redemption. By the war's end in 1814, Sir Thomas (as he now was) had received the thanks of the House of Commons on seven occasions. From 1813 he was a member of that house, having been elected for the Pembroke boroughs. When he was hurriedly recalled to arms in 1815, Picton was as socially settled as a man of his raw temper could be: the master of an estate in Carmarthenshire and a legislator for his country. His death at Waterloo put an end to his short-lived retirement but it ensured his apotheosis. The war hero was revered, the 'blood-soaked governor' of a Caribbean slave island forgotten.

PICTON'S LIFE

1758	Born at Haverfordwest, the son of Thomas Picton, a landowner at Poyston, Pembrokeshire
1771	Begins his military career as a thirteen-year-old ensign with the 12th Foot
1794	A long period of inactivity as a half-pay officer comes to a close when Picton sails for the West Indies
1797	Picton serves in the expedition against Trinidad; he remains on the island as military governor
1803	Picton's dictatorial regime ends when he resigns as governor rather than share authority with civilians. On his arrival in London he is arrested
1806	Picton stands trial in the Court of King's Bench for the abuses of his administration in Trinidad. He is found guilty
1808	At a retrial the jury finds in Picton's favour. He resumes his military career with the expedition to Flushing, Holland, in 1809
1810	Picton joins Wellington's army in Portugal and serves with great distinction for the remainder of the Peninsular War
1812	Buys the 800-acre Iscoed estate in Carmarthenshire for £30,000
1813	Elected MP for the Pembrokeshire boroughs
1814	Napoleon's abdication and exile to Elba. Picton retires to Wales
1815	Dies at the battle of Waterloo

Further reading:
Chris Evans, *Slave Wales: The Welsh and Atlantic Slavery 1660–1850* (2010)

11

IRISH MIGRANTS IN WALES: FRIENDS AND FOES

Paul O'Leary

Ireland's Donncha O' Callaghan (in green) contests possession with Wales's Alun Wyn Jones at Cardiff in 2011

On international day Welsh rugby supporters happily talk of the natural friendship between them and their Irish opponents. We are fellow Celts, they say, and we understand each other instinctively because of our common cultural heritage. Celtic conviviality is the order of the day. Yet, until relatively recently in our history, this idea of a natural kinship between the two nations would have seemed strange and puzzling to both sides. The history of the two peoples is more complicated than the solidarity of international day would suggest.

'VIOLENCE, DECEPTION AND POETRY'

For centuries the Welsh considered the Irish to be an uncivilised people with unfamiliar and unpalatable habits. They looked down their noses at their neighbours on the other side of the sea and their attitudes can be summed up as a mixture of disdain and fear. Take, for example, the radical stonemason, antiquarian and poet Edward Williams (Iolo Morganwg) who wrote in 1799 that 'An Irishman's loves are three: violence, deception and poetry.' He made this dismissive comment not long after the Irish Rebellion of 1798 when well-to-do refugees arrived on the shores of Anglesey and Pembrokeshire in search of temporary hospitality. These newcomers sometimes received a hostile reception from the Welsh and were refused hospitality at inns. This was not an isolated episode.

From the 1820s, Irish migrants began to appear in the new and growing industrial settlements of the country. From the outset they encountered a violent response, as happened at Rhymney in 1826. This was the first major attack on the newcomers, and over the course of the 19th century there would be as many as

Iolo Morganwg, no lover of the Irish

twenty anti-Irish riots across the country, in places as far apart as Cardiff and Holyhead. Ethnic tensions were particularly bad in Monmouthshire and Glamorgan, where the incomers were accused of working for lower wages. In reality there is no concrete evidence to show that the Irish actually undercut the wage rates of native workers and it's likely that the outsiders were simply convenient scapegoats when times were bad. But the reputation stuck.

'PESTILENCE ON THEIR BACKS, FAMINE IN THEIR STOMACHS'

Relations between the two groups deteriorated further during the Irish Great Famine of 1845–50 when about a million Irish peasants starved to death or died of the virulent diseases that thrive in famine conditions. The failure of the potato crop in successive years took away the staple food that sustained millions of poor people. About a million refugees fled the country at this time.

Tens of thousands of these unfortunates arrived at the ports of South Wales after travelling as ballast in the holds of coal ships that returned with a human cargo from Irish ports. Many of these refugees were themselves diseased and starving, and they endured appalling conditions in these sailing ships. Journeys took days or even weeks when the weather was bad, and some refugees died on board ship or succumbed shortly after landing. These were harrowing times when fearful migrants encountered an anxious and sometimes hostile population at their destination. As one commentator

93

at Cardiff put it, the destitute newcomers arrived with nothing more than 'pestilence on their backs, famine in their stomachs'.

Officials in the ports did their best to deter the refugees from landing rather than welcome them. In a vain attempt to stem the flow of people they prosecuted ship captains for carrying too many passengers. The captains responded by avoiding the unpopular reception waiting for them at the main ports and unloaded their human cargo on beaches in small inlets along the coast. In one tragic case in May 1847 an Irishman who had been landed away from the port of Cardiff drowned in the mudflats near Penarth in the face of an oncoming tide. More than two years later the problem remained a pressing one. In June 1849 officials at Cardiff issued a poster advertising a £10 reward for information leading to the conviction of sea captains who landed Irish passengers illegally between Aberthaw and the River Rumney.

The arrival of these refugees coincided with a period of upheaval in towns throughout South Wales as a result of the construction of the South Wales Railway. Major works of this kind brought large numbers of navvies to the area to undertake the gruelling hard work that was necessary to lay the route of the railway, and familiar landscapes were changed by the new form of transport. This made for a heady mix. The combination of the arrival of poor and needy refugees, the outbreak of epidemic disease, the disruption to the local economy, and increased demands on poor relief all created a feeling of urban crisis. And the Irish were fingered as the scapegoats, a group who could be blamed for the bewildering changes taking place. This was exemplified by the riot that broke out at Cardiff in 1849.

The decades after the famine were a difficult time for the Irish community in Wales. Many lived in poverty in the poorest parts of towns, set apart from the rest of society by their distinctive habits and the Catholic religion. They committed a larger proportion of petty crimes than their numbers warranted, and in parts of rural Wales the phrase 'thieving like an Irishman' was in common use at this time. The phrase referred to opportunistic crimes of theft of the kind that were committed by vagrants and provides an insight into how the Irish were perceived.

During the mid-19th century, then, the Irish in Wales were frequently seen as a problem to be solved rather than as Celtic cousins to be embraced.

PROSPERITY AND PROCESSIONS

So how did this situation change? To begin with, we have to remember that not all Irish migrants were poor and needy, even during the famine years.

94

While the majority lacked the kind of skills that might have got them better jobs, a significant minority were employed in skilled occupations and the professions. Some of the Irish at Merthyr, for example, were employed as ironworkers and obtained jobs as 'puddlers'. This was a well-paid occupation that conferred status on those who had the ability and skill to make a success of it and shows that not all Irish migrants were at the base of society.

AN IRISH MERLIN

One Irish individual who achieved prominence in public life was Edward Dowling, the editor of Newport's newspaper, the *Monmouthshire Merlin*, in the 1830s and early 1840s. He used the pages of his newspaper to argue that the Irish in Monmouthshire had not become involved in the Chartist rebellion of November 1839. In fact, some of the Irish had been involved in Chartist activity, but we can interpret Dowling's journalism as his way of showing that the reputation of his fellow countrymen for lawlessness was unjustified.

Irish businessmen achieved prominence in local government. James Murphy became the first Roman Catholic Mayor of Newport in 1868, while John Beirne was the first Irish Mayor of Wrexham in 1877. Cardiff followed with P. J. Carey becoming Mayor of Cardiff in 1894. A sprinkling of Irish doctors were at the centre of medical care in a number of towns and industrial settlements. These medical migrants included Dr Mary Hannan who had worked on medical schemes for women in India and was described in 1896 as 'the first and only Lady Doctor in Wales'. Irish coal merchants and other business people also played a key part in Welsh life.

We need to bear these people in mind when we read contemporaries' statements about 'the low Irish' or the 'poor Irish'. Because the majority of the immigrants arrived at mid-century at a time of acute social and economic change in towns, the attention of many commentators focused on the poorest sections of the Irish community. These were the people who stood out as far as contemporaries were concerned and they represented 'the Irish' as a group to many Welsh people. But we should not make the mistake of thinking that all Irish migrants fitted the stereotype of poor, unskilled and drunken outcasts.

One indicator of this is that from the 1830s a network of Hibernian societies was established in towns across South Wales, beginning in Newport. These organisations were voluntary benefit societies that provided insurance for their members against ill-health, unemployment and death. The societies also had their own bands and took part in public processions through the streets to mark St Patrick's Day, Whitsun, and the ceremonial opening of docks and other public celebrations.

Such occasions were opportunities for some members of the Irish community to demonstrate their 'respectability' to their neighbours. They did this by the way they dressed and behaved. Those taking part in processions wore sober Sunday suits with green sashes and carried banners that proclaimed patriotic Irish sentiments and the loyalty of the Irish to their new homeland. A distinctive feature of the Hibernian societies was that the men wore white trousers with their Sunday-black jackets and green sashes. How you dressed on public occasions in Victorian Wales was meant to convey a strong social and cultural message, and the activities of the Hibernian societies were designed to do exactly that.

Participating in the culture of display in Welsh towns in the 19th century was one avenue for respectable members of the Irish community to demonstrate that they had integrated in local society. Putting yourself on show as part of respectable activities was a way of reassuring other townspeople that the Irish as a group were not a threat.

The *Western Mail* described the 1891 Corpus Christi procession as 'literally the event of the year in the town'

Perhaps the best illustration of this is the annual Catholic Corpus Christi procession that took place in the streets of Cardiff from the mid-1870s. The event was initially sponsored by the Marquis of Bute, a Catholic convert and owner of Cardiff Castle. It consisted of a series of processions of children from the different Catholic parish schools marching to the centre of the town and merging into an enormous procession through the main streets. Their destination was Cardiff Castle, where an open-air service was held in the grounds on the site of a medieval friary. The symbolism of this was clear: the mainly Irish Catholics were linked to the town's highest-status residence (the castle) and to local historic sites that went back centuries. Here, then, was a procession that symbolised the distinctiveness of the Irish community and its integration into local life.

The distinctive feature of the Corpus Christi procession was the large number of young girls dressed in white, and it was this feature of the event that attracted the greatest attention from bystanders and the press. Indeed, by the beginning of the twentieth century about 14,000 girls and boys took part in this impressive and colourful annual procession. It was a far cry from the attitudes that were prevalent during the famine migration half a century earlier. Hibernian parades and Corpus Christi processions showed that it was possible for some Irish people to integrate into life in Welsh towns without rejecting their nationality or religion. The area of Irish life that had the potential to disrupt this development was politics, but even here the Irish succeeded in finding an accommodation with their country of residence.

A UNION OF HEARTS

During the 1860s and early 1870s a revolutionary organisation called the Fenians attracted a great deal of support among Irish migrants. Following the arrest of members of a Fenian cell at Dowlais and Merthyr, there were treason-felony trials at Merthyr and Swansea in the early months of 1868. At this stage the Irish were seen as the enemy within. However, a shift to constitutional politics by the Irish by the 1880s provided new opportunities for the Irish to integrate in local politics. That shift coincided with the rise of the new mass trade unions, which recruited strongly among dockworkers and unskilled labourers, groups that included many Irishmen and women. Irish names were prominent among the officials of these unions in south Wales.

By the mid-1880s South Wales was on the itinerary of visiting Irish nationalist leaders. In June 1886 the leader of the Irish Parliamentary Party, Charles Stuart Parnell, addressed large public meetings at Cardiff and Newport. During his visit to Cardiff he stayed with Dr James Mullin at Cathays, who later revealed that Parnell carried a loaded revolver for his own defence on these speaking tours, though he didn't need it in Wales. Irish nationalist MPs regularly visited Wales and established links with Liberal MPs. At this time politicians began to talk of the 'Union of Hearts' between Irish nationalists and Welsh Liberals.

Sport was another avenue for integration. Before the First World War sporting heroes from the Irish community established themselves as firm favourites with a wider public. The most prominent of these was the boxer 'Peerless' Jim Driscoll, a sportsman who won fame on both sides of the Atlantic. He became Featherweight Champion of Wales in 1901, following this with the British and British Empire Featherweight titles. On the day of his funeral on May 3, 1925, an estimated 100,000 people lined the streets of Cardiff in respectful silence.

WALES AND ELSEWHERE

If we concentrate all our attention on the mid-19th century decades – the time when famine refugees arrived – our picture of Irish migrants is mostly painted in sombre shades. The key features are poverty, disease, high levels of petty crime and alienation. But if we take a longer perspective, other shades of the picture come into focus. When looked at in this light, the experience of Wales looks very different to those of cities such as Liverpool and Glasgow, which had very large Irish communities in the 19th century. Those cities experienced sectarian divides well into the twentieth century, as shown by the bitter rivalry between Glasgow Rangers and Celtic.

In Wales there were small-scale rivalries between Catholics and Protestants, particularly in the field of education where Catholic schools represented a degree of separation. The distress caused by these tensions for individuals and families should not be underestimated. But in general there were none of the bitter, violent and long-lived tensions that continued to scar the public life of Merseyside and the West of Scotland long into the twentieth century. There is some consolation in that conclusion.

Further reading:
Paul O'Leary, *Immigration and Integration: the Irish in Wales, 1798–1922* (2000)

12

ROBERT OWEN: COMMUNITARIAN VISIONARY

Noel Thompson

Between 1815 and 1820, some 20,000 visitors made their way to a cotton mill some four miles from the town of Lanark in Scotland. They came from all parts of Britain, Europe and beyond, and included ambassadors, government ministers, gentry, aristocracy and royalty, including the Grand Duke Nicholas, brother of the Russian Tsar, Alexander. Such industrial tourism was not unheard of but there had been nothing on quite this scale before.

What prompted this influx was not the scenic beauty of its location on the Falls of Clyde, nor the size of the mill; though with around 1,800 employees it was one of the largest of its kind in Britain. What attracted these visitors was a novel social experiment conducted by one of the century's most remarkable men, Robert Owen; an experiment that inspired the enthusiasm and admiration of contemporaries and, for a time, gave its originator easy access to the great and the good.

A statue of Robert Owen in the centre of Newtown

Modern-day Newtown

THE SELF-MADE MAN

In many ways Robert Owen was the epitome of the 19th-century ideal of the self-made man. He was born in Newtown, Montgomeryshire, the son of a saddler and ironmonger (Robert Owen) and a farmer's daughter (Anne Williams) on May 14, 1771; became apprenticed at the age of ten to James McGuffog, a cloth manufacturer in Stamford, Lincolnshire; moved in 1784 to work for a London retailer before moving again to Manchester, where he set up a company to manufacture equipment for making thread, before, at the age of 21, becoming the manager of Drinkwater's, a major mill with 500 employees.

Then, in the kind of career move beloved of writers of fiction, he married Ann Caroline Dale, the daughter of David Dale, a successful mill owner, purchasing that mill in 1800 on favourable terms for £60,000 and assuming the role of manager. Under his control it proved an immensely profitable concern but it was not that which brought visitors to New Lanark from across the globe but rather the new principles which he applied to the organisation and treatment of the workforce.

THE LAIRD OF NEW LANARK

The workforce that he inherited at New Lanark was, despite David Dale's best efforts, a fairly motley crew, described by Owen as 'idle, intemperate, dishonest and devoid of truth'. It was comprised of some 500 orphan or pauper apprentices from institutions or parishes in Glasgow and Edinburgh, a considerable number of young women, and migrants from the decaying economy of the Highlands.

The problems that confronted Owen were those that might be expected given the community's composition: pilfering, vandalism, sexual misconduct, drunkenness, ill-discipline and general unruliness; behaviour that necessarily had adverse consequences for the productivity and profitability of the enterprise. His achievement was to transform it and the mill's profitability in ways that seized the interest and imagination of his contemporaries.

During his time as manager of New Lanark, hours were shortened, no child under the age of ten was employed in the mill and provision was made

100

for sickness and old age; the company store was stocked with quality goods at reasonable prices and, most importantly, Owen developed a system of infant education through an Institute for the Formation of Character that was opened in 1816. Natural history, geography, daily dancing and singing and military exercises were all integral to the curriculum. There were zoological and mineralogical specimens to inform the lessons and excite the interest of the children, with a stuffed crocodile pride of place amongst this collection. There was also an absence of corporal punishment, with kindness to the children being a guiding principle.

CHILDREN: 'WONDERFULLY CONTRIVED COMPOUNDS'

The principles which Owen applied to effect his radical change were set out in a volume entitled *Essays on the principle of the formation of human character (1813–14)*. The underlying message of the work was clearly stated by Owen himself: 'the character of man is, without a single exception, always formed for him', with children seen as 'passive and wonderfully contrived compounds; which… may be ultimately moulded into the very image of rational wishes and desires'. It was this belief that informed his efforts: the belief that people could be transformed by transforming their working and educational environment.

As to the mill itself, the aim was to create a well-organised and disciplined labour force. To this end, and amongst other expedients, Owen used a 'silent monitor' or 'telegraph', described by Owen himself as 'a four-sided piece of wood... each side coloured – one side black, another blue, the third yellow and the fourth white', 'suspended in a conspicuous place near to each of the persons employed' with 'the colour at the front telling the conduct of the individual during the preceding day to four degrees of comparison'. Each day's publicly displayed colour was then entered in a 'book of character', which Owen likened to that of the recording angel on the Day of Judgement.

THE SOCIALIST VISIONARY

Owen seemed a man in harmony with the spirit of the age: a successful industrialist, an educator, a philanthropist, a social reformer; someone who took seriously his duties to his employees and to society. And so having attracted near universal acclaim for what he had achieved, Owen sought to use the New Lanark model as the basis for addressing the contemporary blight of poverty and social deprivation.

To do so, Owen looked to create largely self-sufficient 'villages of union and mutual co-operation' of between 500 and 1500 people, situated in a rural environment but making use of machinery where appropriate. Here were all the benefits of industry but with a population removed from the filth, squalor and pollution of the urban environment in which industry was usually located: a New Lanark built again and again in a green and pleasant land. A self-contained, local experiment now became a national programme of social transformation.

It is at this juncture that, for many of those previously generous with their plaudits, the hero began to assume some of the characteristics of a villain. Owen's broad aim of radical social change was one reason but there were others.

From an early age, Owen tells us in his autobiography, he had believed that there was 'something fundamentally wrong with all religions'. As long as such religious scepticism remained a private matter there was no problem. But as Owen began to encounter opposition to his wider schemes for social reform, so he began to see the Church and its doctrines as a major obstacle to that change in men's minds that was required to usher in what he increasingly termed a 'new moral world'. In particular Owen was incensed at what he saw as the clergy's attempts to undermine his efforts, in 1817, to secure a Factory Act to limit the hours worked by children in factories. And at a public meeting at the City of London Tavern in August 1817 he lambasted their doctrines as having made man 'a weak, imbecile animal; a furious bigot and fanatic; or a miserable hypocrite'. The love affair with a critical element of the British Establishment began to turn a little sour.

Even more dangerous and provocative was the way in which he began in this period to think and write about the lifeblood of the economic system – profits. For, as he was coming to see it, the pursuit of profit – the competition it produced, the treatment of labour it promoted and the morally dubious behaviour inherent in commercial activity – was at the heart of the impoverishment and social malaise that characterised industrial society.

Moreover competition and the competitive spirit, which many con-temporaries saw as the driver of the economic system, were now roundly condemned. For Owen they made for social antagonism, pitting individual against individual and class against class, and encouraged immoral and selfish behaviour degrading to humanity.

By the 1820s, Owen was also increasingly insisting that labour was the foundation of all value: an idea to which he was to give practical expression in a National Equitable Labour Exchange established in Gray's Inn Road in London in 1832 where goods were exchanged for labour notes denominated in hours of work.

At this time too he began voicing critical views of marriage and what it entailed, which together with the notion of communal living was a major cause for concern amongst many who would previously have applauded the improvement of character at the heart of the New Lanark experiment.

As to his villages of union, these were now increasingly seen as communities of property and goods where those who laboured could reap the fruits of their efforts free from the depredations of greedy employers and rack-renting landlords, and where an environment could be created that would form characters qualitatively different and superior to any that existed in the old immoral world.

To all intents and purposes, therefore, the self-made business man and educational reformer was becoming a socialist with a revolutionary take on the world's ills and how they might be remedied. His message was no longer simply that of improving the lot of the working classes, but the emancipation of mankind by radical means. His had now become a dissonant voice no longer in harmony with the spirit of the age. The hero had become a villain.

THE HERO OF THE WORKING CLASSES

But if Owen had become a villain for prelates, politicians, profit seekers and political economists, he was beginning to assume the role of hero for those whose interests he increasingly saw himself as advancing. If the Establishment bridled at the notion of communities and community of property, many amongst the working classes warmed to this idea. Initially there were doubts about Owen's schemes for self-sufficient communities. Some referred to them as 'parallelograms of paupers' but gradually a more positive view came to prevail.

It was in 1825 that Owen made the first attempt turn his vision of a new moral world into the reality of a co-operative community characterized by united labour, expenditure and property. Such a community, he believed, had to be removed from the pervasive corruption of the old order and so a township and estate of 20,000 acres was purchased in Indiana from a German Pietist sect, the Rappites, and the co-operative community of New Harmony was born in Indiana on the banks of the Wabash River. However, the experiment lasted only a short time. By late 1827/early 1828 the community had effectively disintegrated, consuming a substantial part of Owen's fortune in the process. But this did not dampen his enthusiasm and that of others for the communitarian ideal.

In Britain, Owen's ideas took root and acquired a following. And when he returned in the late 1820s it was to a country with some 300 co-operative societies and where his ideas were being developed by other socialist thinkers.

Moreover they were finding their way into a trade union movement which, in the early 1830s, was embroiled in a period of intense industrial conflict. With characteristic energy, Owen threw himself into the fray, establishing a newspaper, *The Crisis*, in 1832, and playing a major role in creating a general union that spanned all trades – the short-lived Grand National Consolidated Trades Union.

After its collapse in 1834, Owen went on to form the Association of All Classes of All Nations that became the University Community Society of Rational Religionists (or, in short, the Rational Society) with over 60 branches and a paper called the *New Moral World*, 1834–45 that disseminated Owenite ideas on communitarian socialism to an audience that included the young Friedrich Engels, working in the 1840s for a branch of the family firm in Manchester.

Owen's ideas therefore found a broad constituency. The villain of the Establishment had become the hero of the Labour Movement. He had become, and remained, an inspiration for those who sought, through practical means such as co-operative wholesale societies, as well as more ambitious schemes, such as co-operative communities, to transform the lot of labour. One further attempt was made by him to create a new moral order with the establishment of a community at Queenwood, near Tytherley, in Hampshire, in 1839, but it failed, bankrupting the Rational Society in the process.

Thereafter Owen and Owen's ideas did not generate the same kind of interest as they had in the 1820s and 1830s, though enthusiasm for them increased markedly during the socialist revival of the 1880s and 1890s and his ideas on co-operation and community undoubtedly inspired the co-operative wholesale movement that grew rapidly in the 19th and early 20th centuries.

THE 'FERTILE-BRAINED WELSHMAN'

But what of his reputation in Wales?

Owen visited Wales only twice after leaving Newtown to pursue his career, before returning to die at the Bear's Head Hotel on November 17, 1858. Yet he spent the first ten years of his life in this bustling market town and it would be wrong to underestimate the influence that his Welsh upbringing had upon him. Indeed his most recent biographer, Ian Donnachie, has been at pains to emphasize it.

It was also the case that two co-operative communities were established in Wales, both by organisations inspired

His own character and outlook...were shaped by his Welsh roots, by his Welsh linguistic and cultural heritage, by the Welshness of his schooling and his religious upbringing, by his immediate family and kin, and by the environment of Montgomeryshire, specifically of Newtown and it's surroundings.

Ian Donnachie

104

by Owen's thinking: the first, Pant Glas, near Abergeirw in Meirionnydd in 1839, by members of the Liverpool-based Society of United Friends, and the second, Garn Lwyd, eight miles south east of Carmarthen in the Gwendraeth Fach valley in 1848, by members of the Leeds Redemption Society. Neither lasted long: Pant Glas until 1840 and Garn Lwyd, a little longer until it folded some time in 1853 or 1854.

Robert Owen's grave at St Mary's, Newtown

Yet it was to be some time before Wales and Newtown showed any marked appreciation of one of their most famous sons. In 1861 an offer from the Co-operative Union to put a marble tombstone on his grave was refused by Newtown's worthies. Disinterest or hostility were often the reaction that his name provoked, with inhabitants taking little pride in what Owen had achieved and the global reputation he had built. As with the British Establishment, so with the burghers of Newtown, his aberrant ideas about religion, marriage, community of property and goods, and communal living had made him, if not a villain, then someone over whose association with the town it was thought best to draw a veil. Indeed it was not until 1956 that a memorial statue was erected with funds raised by the Labour and Co-operative Movement at the intersection of Short Bridge Street and Gas Street.

Yet there were those in Wales who did recognize his greatness and who put him amongst the pantheon of Welsh heroes. In 1892 Tom Ellis, the Liberal M.P. for Meirionnydd, gave an address to Bangor University students. In it he looked at four categories of Welsh hero defining the last of these as 'those who have pondered over the outlook for the social well-being of man, of the relation of man to man, the bearers of the *Neges Cymru*'. And in that category he put Robert Owen, as 'a strong, strenuous, fertile-brained Welshman' to be ranked with Plato and Sir Thomas More. The *Neges Cymru* ('the message of Wales') which Owen brought to the world was one that sprang from a society characterized by the ideals of co-operation, mutual assistance and social solidarity. It was these ideals that had informed Owen's life, work and thought, and it was these which, Ellis believed, had been taken by Owen from Wales to the wider world.

Further reading:

N. Thompson and C. Williams (eds), *Robert Owen and his Legacy* (2011)

13

LORD TREDEGAR: ONE OF TENNYSON'S 'SIX HUNDRED'

Chris Williams

Today he sits in statued form, astride his charger Sir Briggs, his back to City Hall, overlooking Cardiff's busy Boulevard de Nantes. Most of those who drive past will barely give him a second glance.

Statue of Lord Tredegar outside City Hall, Cardiff

Less than a century ago, when in 1913 he died at the age of 81, Godfrey Charles Morgan, Viscount Tredegar, was acclaimed as Wales's 'most distinguished citizen' by the Liberal *South Wales Daily News*. Its rival, the Conservative *Western Mail*, agreed, stating that Morgan 'filled a great place in public affairs... there never was a nobleman who attracted to himself such a wealth of affectionate esteem.'

What did Lord Tredegar do to merit such tributes? Why was he being remembered in W. Goscombe John's statuary in 1909, before his death? Was he then, and is he now, a Welsh hero?

BALACLAVA: THE MAKING OF A HERO

In order to answer such questions we must start in April 1831, when Godfrey was born at the now-ruined Ruperra Castle, roughly equidistant between Cardiff and Newport. He was the second son of Sir Charles Morgan Robinson and his wife Rosamund. Sir Charles was heir to the Tredegar estate which owned much of Newport, a good part of Cardiff, and extensive tracts of land and industrial properties in the coalfield.

As befitted one of the wealthiest families in Wales, Godfrey was educated at Eton College. After leaving aged 17, like many second sons in the landed classes he joined the forces, being commissioned into the cavalry regiment, the 17th Lancers, known as the 'Death or Glory Boys'. By 1853, when war between Turkey and Russia broke out, Godfrey was a captain, and when Britain and France entered the conflict in March 1854, the 17th Lancers were sent to the Crimean peninsula in the Black Sea. Godfrey's younger brother Frederick, a captain in the Rifle Brigade, was also on his way to war. As their eldest brother Charles Rodney had died earlier that year (leaving Godfrey heir), there was a real prospect that Sir Charles (who had inherited the Tredegar estate in 1846) and his wife could lose three sons in one year.

Stormed at with shot and shell,
Boldly they rode and well,
Into the jaws of Death,
Into the mouth of Hell
Rode the six hundred.

Lines from Alfred Lord Tennyson's 'The Charge of the Light Brigade'

Lord Tredegar's birthplace, Ruperrra Castle

British and French troops landed on the Crimea in September 1854 and within a week had fought a major battle at the Alma (a name today preserved in occasional pub signs, street names, and as a rare Christian name – Alma Cogan anyone?). With the Russians subsequently behind their defences in the port of Sevastopol, the Allies made the small harbour of Balaclava their base.

On October 25 the Russians launched an attack on Allied positions outside Balaclava. The battle contained three noteworthy encounters: the repulse of a Russian cavalry attack by the 'Thin Red Line' of the 93rd Highlanders; the extremely successful Charge of the Heavy Brigade of British cavalry which routed a much superior Russian mounted force; and the notorious, glorious Charge of the Light Brigade.

This is not the place to revisit the controversies associated with the infamous Charge, about which much has been written. Tony Richardson's 1968 film starring John Gielgud as Lord Raglan, Harry Andrews as Lord Lucan (no, not that one) and Trevor Howard as Lord Cardigan is worth an evening of your time if you wish to refresh your memory and relax simultaneously. Alternatively, George MacDonald Fraser's comic novel *Flashman at the Charge* is an amusing and provocative commentary on this episode and on history writing in general.

Lord Tredegar's steed, Sir Briggs, is buried beneath this obelisk at Tredegar House

What we know for certain is that the Light Brigade, comprised of the 13th Light Dragoons, the 17th Lancers, the 11th Hussars, the 8th Hussars and the 4th Light Dragoons, and totalling 673 officers and men, was ordered to attack Russian positions at the end of the North Valley. To reach the enemy it had to advance approximately two kilometres exposed not only to frontal fire from Russian artillery batteries, but also to flanking fire from more guns on left and right.

So, with 'cannon to right of them, cannon to left of them, cannon to front of them' the cavalry moved off at about 11am. Captain Godfrey Morgan on Sir Briggs was in the front line and witnessed the death of the impetuous (and possibly culpable) Captain Nolan, but had no time to mourn him as the advance proceeded 'amidst the thickest shower of shell, shot, grape, canister, and minie, from front and flanks – horses and men dropping by scores every yard' (as Morgan wrote to his father after the battle).

Remarkably, the Light Brigade reached the Russian positions, but suffering heavy losses had no option but to turn around and retreat. At this point Morgan was almost cut off, but 'digging my spurs in my horse's sides, he went at it as he has often gone at the big fences in Monmouthshire' and made it back to British lines.

Godfrey was one of only two officers in the 17th Lancers to return unscathed. Of the 673 who began the charge, 113 had been killed, 134 wounded and 15 taken prisoners. As important, 475 of the horses were dead. Although the Light Brigade saw further action in the last major battle of the war, at Inkerman on November 5, it had been rendered almost impotent.

HOME AND GLORY

The French General Pierre Bosquet, after witnessing the Charge of the Light Brigade, reputedly exclaimed 'C'est magnifique, mais ce n'est pas la guerre: c'est de la folie' ('it is magnificent, but it is not war: it is madness'). Perhaps Godfrey Morgan would have agreed with him, as in a letter written to his mother on November 7 he declared himself 'heartily sick of these fearful scenes of carnage and bloodshed... one's best friends mowed down day after day'. Soon after, like so many on campaign, he fell ill (more than three times as many British troops died from disease in the Crimea as from enemy action) and was hospitalised at Scutari, although we do not know whether he was attended to by Florence Nightingale.

In January 1855, Godfrey was gazetted out of the army. He explained that his father 'thought that one such action [as Balaclava] was sufficient to prove the mettle of his son'. Both he and his horse returned to the family home at Tredegar House, Sir Briggs living until 1874. Today Godfrey's steed is buried beneath a memorial obelisk in the Cedar Garden, next to another marking the last resting place of his favourite Skye terrier 'Peeps'.

Although Godfrey's active military career was now over, he did serve as a major in the Royal Gloucestershire Yeomanry, later becoming Honorary Colonel of the Royal Monmouthshire Royal Engineers and President of the Monmouth Territorial Force Association.

Clearly, Balaclava was an association that brought him lifelong fame. He regularly hosted anniversary dinners at Tredegar House, and attended gatherings of Light Brigade survivors for the rest of his life. He was justifiably proud of his involvement in the iconic 'Charge' and as late as 1905 commissioned his favourite portrait artist, John Charlton, to produce a scene of him in the thick of the action.

Yet in public Morgan was more modest. He felt that 'my own courage in the memorable charge was small' and noted that 'the term "hero" is a term with which many soldiers do not agree'. He recalled Rudyard Kipling's poem 'Tommy' with its line 'We aren't no thin red 'eroes, nor we aren't no blackguards too'.

PARLIAMENT, POLITICS AND THE PEERAGE

Godfrey Morgan's return to civilian life involved taking on the responsibilities of (as he had become) the heir to the Tredegar estate. It was usual for Morgans to sit in Parliament, and in December 1858 he was elected unopposed as Conservative MP for the county of Brecon, sitting in Parliament for the next seventeen years, and occasionally residing in Brecon's Mansion House.

As was quite common in 19th-century Wales, Godfrey was returned unopposed at the next three general elections (1859, 1865 and 1868) before comfortably defeating a Liberal opponent (William Fuller-Maitland, a famous cricketer, who would in due course serve as Breconshire's MP) in 1874.

In 1859, Godfrey's father, Sir Charles, was raised to the peerage as Baron Tredegar, an objective for which the Morgans had been striving for some decades. This would normally have been the ideal moment for Godfrey to marry and start producing further heirs, but although he had been betrothed when he left for the Crimea in 1854, during his absence his fiancée had married another man. Godfrey remained a lifelong bachelor, though maintaining a close relationship with the lady in question for many decades.

In 1875 Baron Tredegar died, and Godfrey was raised to the peerage and thus to the House of Lords. He remained, as he put it, 'naturally Conservative', and served as President of the South Monmouthshire and Newport Conservative Associations. But he rarely attended Parliament and entertained some idiosyncratic views – unusually for a Conservative peer he was in favour of women's suffrage.

Instead he focused his public service locally: as Lord Lieutenant of Breconshire and of Monmouthshire, as a magistrate for Breconshire and Glamorgan, as a county councillor, alderman and eventually (1902–3) chairman of Monmouthshire County Council.

As Lord Tredegar, Morgan was a landlord with extensive properties. Landowners in general tend not to enjoy a good press in Welsh history, as they are associated with putting political pressure on tenants to vote in particular ways, being frequently accused of absenteeism, exploitation and fostering 'English' values.

In Morgan's defence one might note that his first contested election took place after the introduction in 1872 of the secret ballot, that apart from six weeks each summer he lived in South Wales, and that although his command of the Welsh tongue was at best rudimentary, he continued his family's historic associations with Welsh culture, sponsoring many *eisteddfodau*.

On the 'question of Monmouthshire' he was usually in favour of the 'Welsh solution', although he acknowledged before an audience of Newport rugby players in 1891 that Monmouthshire was 'a sort of hybrid county' and that 'Cardiff is very jealous of us … because we can get drunk on Sundays and they can't' (following the introduction of Sunday Closing to Wales but not to Monmouthshire in 1881). Mischievously, he supported the idea of a Monmouthshire Parliament at Newport!

As a landlord, Morgan enjoyed a reputation for generosity and solicitude towards his tenants. At times of agricultural depression he issued rent rebates of between 10 and 20 per cent. He drew explicit praise (as a 'Good Samaritan') for his treatment of his lessees from witnesses to the 1894 Royal Commission on the Land in Wales and Monmouthshire.

Like his forefathers, Morgan took a strong interest in the promotion of agricultural methods. He continued the Tredegar Agricultural Show, bred livestock and shire horses on his estate, and was President of the (now Royal) Smithfield Club, the (now Royal) Bath and West of England Society, the (then) Royal Agricultural Society, the Shire Horse Society and the Hackney Horse Society.

The Tredegar Estate was also a commercial and industrial one, and Morgan was chairman of Newport's Alexandra Docks company and of the town's Chamber of Commerce. He hailed the port's potential as 'a second Liverpool' and also played a considerable part in the development of Cardiff.

Morgan frequently made gifts of land for the building of churches (both Anglican and Nonconformist), schools, libraries, hospitals and parks. Major benefactions include sites of the University College in Cardiff, the Royal Gwent Hospital in Newport and the Rodney Parade site of the Newport Athletic Club. All told, his public benefactions were estimated to amount to £40,000 a year.

I am not accustomed to begging, being more accustomed to being begged of. That is one of the hereditary privileges of members of the House of Lords.

Morgan at a meeting in connection with the new Infirmary for Newport, March 17, 1897

He is a very attractive old man, with a sparkle of fun in his blue eyes and a thorough Grand Seigneur *of ancient days in his appearance and manner.*

Walburga Lady Paget, *In My Tower* (1924), on her visit to Tredegar House in 1895

111

THE 'GRAND OLD MAN OF THE PRINCIPALITY'

A keen sportsman in his younger days, Morgan was an accomplished steeplechaser and cricketer. For forty years he was master of the Tredegar Hunt, and also took a strong interest in bowls, fishing, grouse shooting, hockey and 'any and every manly sport'. In later life he developed a passion for archaeology and antiquarianism, serving as president of the Cambrian Archaeological Association. He also dressed up as Owen Glyndwr (that was the contemporary spelling) for the National Pageant of Wales in 1909.

Morgan lived alone (that is, apart from a small army of servants!) and unostentatiously in the very ostentatious Tredegar House. The architectural historian John Newman calls it 'the grandest and most exuberant country house in the county, and one of the most outstanding of the Restoration period in the whole of Britain', but Morgan was not interested in innovations such as gas or electric lighting, the telephone, or the motor car.

In December 1905, Baron Tredegar was raised to the Viscountcy as a mark of public esteem for his long years of public service. To be more cynical, it

Lord Tredegar as 'Owen Glyndwr' in the National Pageant of Wales, 1909

was also a gesture of recognition by an outgoing Conservative government hopeful of retaining the South Monmouthshire parliamentary seat (held by Godfrey's brother Frederick) in the forthcoming general election. In this regard it did not succeed, but further tributes to Godfrey followed in his last years.

Almost seven thousand people subscribed to a Monmouthshire testimonial to him prompted by 'the treatment of your tenants during agricultural depression' and in 1909 he was given the freedom of the boroughs of both Newport and Cardiff (the occasion for the erection of the equestrian statue in Cathays Park).

Through his extensive philanthropy and patronage of many local societies, Morgan was in much demand as an after-dinner speaker and 'inveterate bazaar opener'. He calculated that, in laying foundation stones, he had amassed a collection of trowels and mallets sufficient to equip every parish church in the country.

He developed a reputation for amusing and enlightening speeches, which often drew on his passion for poetry (favourites being Wordsworth as well as the aforementioned Tennyson and Kipling). One biographer termed him the 'Mark Twain of Wales'. In 1911 the *Western Mail* published a collection – *The Wit and Wisdom of Lord Tredegar* – with illustrations by the leading cartoonist J. M. Staniforth.

At about this time Godfrey Morgan's health began to fail. He died on March 11, 1913, of influenza and is buried in St Basil's Church, Bassaleg, not far from his family home. The viscountcy became extinct, and the barony and baronetcy passed to his nephew, Courtenay Charles Evan Morgan. The great days of the house of Tredegar were over: the Morgans would never again enjoy such prosperity and renown, nor exert such influence in the affairs of South Wales.

Was Godfrey Charles Morgan a hero? For his part in the battle of Balaclava, the answer must be yes, although that is only a small part of his story. What his later life reveals is rather more significant in the context of the history of Wales. Here was an Anglican, a landowner and a Tory who nonetheless occupied a secure niche in the affections of the Welsh people. He was a hero of his time, if not of ours. Perhaps the fact that he is now largely forgotten is a tribute to progress. For as Bertolt Brecht stated: 'unhappy the land that needs heroes.'

CHRONOLOGY

1831	Born, Ruperra Castle
1853	Commissioned into 17th Lancers
1854	Charge of the Light Brigade
1855	Returns to Newport
1858	Elected Conservative MP for Breconshire
1875	Becomes Baron Tredegar
1905	Becomes Viscount Tredegar
1909	Receives Freedom of the Boroughs of Newport and Cardiff
1913	Dies April 11, of influenza, at Tredegar House

Further reading:
Lord Tredegar, *The Wit and Wisdom of Lord Tredegar* (1911) [available online]

14

WILLIAM ROBERT GROVE: THE SCIENTIST AS HERO

Iwan Rhys Morus

SHOWDOWN AT SWANSEA

On August 9, 1848, the jamboree that was the annual meeting of the British Association for the Advancement of Science arrived in Swansea. It was the first time the association had set foot in Wales – and on its 18th birthday too. And there had clearly been doubts about the prospect on the part of the scientific gentlemen. The previous year a delegation had been dispatched to damp down fears that Swansea might not be quite the right town for the British Ass. They had nothing to worry about as things turned out. The nervous delegation reported back that 'suitable accommodation for the public purposes of the Association could be found in the Royal Institution, the Assembly Rooms, the Town Hall, Theatre, and certain large school-rooms.' The locals were inclined to be friendly, they reported too. So comforted, the gentlemen of science decided that Swansea would do after all.

The man behind all of this was William Robert Grove. It was Grove who had delivered Swansea's invitation to the BAAS as they gathered at Southampton in 1846. In 1847 he was the man tasked with making sure the inspecting committee went away convinced that Swansea could do the job. A great deal rested on this visit. The British Ass was an institution that mattered. A visit from them was a real sign of prestige. It was a sign that a town had made it – the culmination of civic ambition. In some ways this was the beginning of Swansea's bid to be recognized as the Welsh metropolis. The great and the good of British science gathered for these occasions. Hopeful provincials could mingle with metropolitan scientific gentlemen or Cambridge and Oxford professors. The association's annual proceedings were widely reported in the press. Audiences packed into crowded halls to hear about the latest discoveries – and the scientific gossip. They went on philosophical picnics and geo-botanical rambles.

Grove was the 'potent magician' who had made it all happen. That at least was what the Marquis of Northampton said in his presidential address. It was – and must have been meant as – a double-edged compliment. It was a bit of cheek really, calling a successful London barrister a 'representative of the Bard and Druid of ancient Britain.' It was certainly meant to remind him of his proper place. Northampton, as we shall see, had reason enough to do Grove down in that summer of revolutions in 1848. Grove had just cost the Marquis his own throne as President of the Royal Society. But Grove probably did not worry too much about Northampton's bad manners. His campaign

William Robert Grove

to bring the British Ass home to Swansea had been successful. He had put Wales on the scientific map. In London, he was at the forefront of what looked like some real scientific revolutions as well – just as momentous as the political ones taking place across the channel.

Historians of science now remember Grove mainly for two things. First, his theory of the correlation of physical forces, often cited as an important precursor of the conservation of energy. Second, his invention of the gas battery – or the fuel cell as we now call it. Both theory and battery were products of Grove's tenure as Professor of Experimental Philosophy at the London Institution during the first half of the 1840s. Those five years were the pinnacle of Grove's scientific career. They demonstrate too how difficult it was – even for someone like Grove – to make a career out of science. Grove abandoned his professorship and returned to the law for one simple reason. He could not afford to remain as a man of science. He can certainly be painted as a scientific hero (though the Marquis of Northampton might disagree) but was he really a Welsh hero too?

WELSH SCIENCE?

Grove had been born in Swansea on July 11, 1811. His father, John, was a prosperous local magistrate and deputy lieutenant of the county. He went to the local grammar school and a private tutor in Bath before setting off for Brasenose College, Oxford, in 1830. His father had wanted the young Grove to enter the church. Grove himself had different ideas though. He was called to the Bar in 1835. Ill health (which had probably kept him out of the clutches of public school) kept him out of active legal practice throughout the 1830s.

Instead, he went on a Grand Tour of the Continent – and revived a youthful enthusiasm for electrical experiments.

Even though Grove's brief scientific career mostly took place in London, I want to try to paint him into a thoroughly Welsh picture here. I think that it's important to do this simply because we do not usually think of ourselves in Wales as having much to do with science. We're a land of hymns and arias, preachers and poets. But Grove's career should remind us of something that most of us probably never knew. Wales in the first half of the 19th century had a vibrant scientific culture. Grove was one of its products and one of its promoters. From the 1830s onwards, local scientific societies popped up all over Wales. They came in all shapes and sizes. Some were quite prestigious in their day, like the Royal Institution of South Wales, of which Grove was such a prominent member. Others, like the Literary and Scientific Societies of Aberystwyth or Cardigan came and went rather more quietly.

One of the earliest of these ventures – unsurprisingly perhaps – was the Swansea Literary and Scientific Institution. Hot on its heels came similar institutions in Merthyr, Cardiff, Neath and Pontypridd. Beyond the heavily industrializing south, they sprung up in Carmarthen, Llangefni, Tenby and Haverfordwest. Local enthusiasts offered scientific papers and collections of instruments or specimens. Proceedings were mainly in English but at least occasionally in Welsh – particularly when aimed at improving the minds of the working classes. Touring lecturers passed through Welsh towns with their active little scientific societies in a regular circuit. They offered earnest discussions of astronomy, chemistry – and electricity of course. They offered lectures on physiology to promote the benefits of teetotalism. Less earnestly maybe, crowds gathered to hear and see the latest scientific fads of mesmerism and phrenology.

Grove cut his own scientific teeth at these sorts of societies. They provided the culture that fed his revived enthusiasm for matters electric. He was one of the eleven founder members of the Swansea Literary and Scientific Institution in 1835. He was instrumental as well in its transformation into the Royal Institution of South Wales three years later. There he forged contacts with prominent industrialists and well-connected scientific enthusiasts like Lewis Weston Dillwyn and John Henry Vivian. They in turn did their best to push him along in his scientific life. Grove was back and forth between London and Swansea during these years. He clearly kept his Swansea backers up to date with his scientific activities. In 1839 he offered 'an account of some new electro-chemical experiments' to the Royal Institution of South Wales audience. It was in Swansea and in constant touch with his scientific circle there that he started serious work on his ground-breaking batteries. They helped shape his scientific ethos too.

BATTERY POWER

Electricity was Grove's real passion by now. Electricity really seemed like the future in the 1830s. Enthusiasts claimed that it would soon replace steam as the power propelling the British Empire forwards. The nitric acid battery that Grove invented in 1839 would soon become the standard power source for the electric telegraph industry.

THE GREATEST POWER IN THE SMALLEST SPACE

When Grove announced his new battery to the world, it was typical that he made great play of its industrial potential. 'As it seems probable that at no very distant period voltaic electricity may become useful as a means of locomotion, the arrangement of the batteries so as to produce the greatest power in the smallest space, becomes important,' he said. As well as batteries, Grove spent his time investigating producing light by electricity – useful in mines, he speculated. He even came up with a clever way of etching copies of daguerreotype plates with electricity.

Looking back, we would now see the gas battery – the fuel cell that seems set to save the car industry – as the key invention that came out of this remarkably productive flurry of experiment. The principle behind the gas battery was simple enough. Grove found that oxygen and hydrogen combined on a platinum surface to generate a current. As far as he was concerned at the time, though, it was only one of a number of fascinating demonstrations of the power and versatility of electricity. A neat trick was to use the electricity generated by the gas battery to decompose water into oxygen and hydrogen. The gases could then be recombined on platinum to give water and the electric current back again. This was, said Grove, 'a beautiful instance of the correlation of natural forces.' It was a clever way of making visible the way chemical and electrical forces were forever producing each other.

That was what Grove had in mind with his theory of the correlation of physical forces. You could never say, he said, that any one force caused any one other. In the right circumstances any force could be exploited to produce another. Electricity could make light and light could make electricity. What correlation demonstrated was not just that science was meant to be useful, it showed that usefulness was built into the natural order of things. It was all about production and exchange. I might almost call this a theory made in Wales and delivered from the professor's podium at the London Institution. It was the result of Grove's musing over the significance of his electrical experiments. It was also, no doubt, well informed by discussions with the hard industrial men who dominated the Royal Institution of South Wales.

SCIENTIFIC REFORM

Right from the beginning of his tenure at the London Institution, Grove was making it plain that science was meant to be at the service of industry. His inaugural lecture, where the seeds of correlation first appeared, celebrated the union of science and commerce. The fiery Welshman was clearly not too impressed by what he saw of the state of science in London, however. An anonymous article he penned for *Blackwood's Magazine* in 1843 laid into the scientific establishment with real venom. Too many of the leading lights of London science were in it for 'petty gain and class celebrity.' They were out 'to convert science into pounds, shillings and pence' whilst kicking the ladder of success away from under 'the poor aspirants who attempt to follow them'. No wonder it was an anonymous article!

Clearly happy to get his hands dirty in the right cause, Grove was soon in the thick of it. Made a Fellow of the Royal Society in 1840, it did not take him long to get his feet under the table as a member of Council. Once there he was quite ready to make trouble. A new breed of men of science (many, like Grove, with links to industry and commerce) had been agitating to reform the grand dame of British science for decades. Grove joined their ranks and pushed through his own proposed reforms with dogged and characteristic perseverance. No more dilettantes and unqualified aristocrats was the gist of Grove's proposals, along with strict limits (fifteen a year) on the number of Fellows that could be elected. The old guard – with the Marquis of Northampton as President of the Royal Society in their vanguard – were furious. But for once Grove and his fellow conspirators had the Council packed with their supporters and the reformers got their way at last in February 1847.

It was still not the end of the battle for the Royal Society's soul. Grove was put up to replace the tarnished Peter Mark Roget as one of the society's Secretaries. Northampton in his presidential address to the Fellows at the end of the year washed his hands of the reforms. The writing was clearly on the wall for his tenure as president now as well. As Grove rushed back and forth between London and Swansea during the opening months of 1848, he had to juggle his own candidacy for the secretaryship with the need to ensure a smoothly run and uncontentious meeting of the British Ass that summer. It was a tall order, but Grove managed it. The Swansea meeting was a triumph. Grove's own battle for the secretaryship of the Royal Society was less triumphant. The reactionaries rallied and he lost.

Grove certainly packed a lot into the decade or so for which he was an active man of science. He had resigned his London professorship in 1846 and returned to the Bar. His catastrophic defeat over the secretaryship led to a marked decline in his participation in the Royal Society's affairs as well. His legal career prospered instead. He was a QC by the mid-1850s and ended his career at last as a judge in the Court of Common Pleas. He sat on Royal Commissions (on sewers and on patents). He made a few further interventions in science. He was President of the British Association for the Advancement of Science for its meeting in Birmingham in 1866. And during his presidential address, he became the first British Association president to announce his support for Darwin's theory of evolution by means of natural selection.

A SCIENTIFIC HERO

All of which brings us back to Swansea and the British Association meeting of 1848. We can count Grove as a Welsh hero – as well as a scientific one – because what he did there was remind his gentlemanly fellow savants that Wales had its own scientific culture too. His success on the metropolitan scientific stage probably reminded some of his fellow Welshmen of the fact too. Grove did not need to leave Wales to find science. Its culture of earnest enthusiasm was there for him already. Some Victorian gentlemen of science (like Darwin in his early geologizing) treated Wales as a sort of *terra incognita* – a playground for competing theories. Grove at Swansea showed them that Wales deserved a place on the scientific map in a different way.

Northampton's sly compliments were typical of the way Wales was often dismissed as quaint but irrelevant by the Victorian metropolitan elite. Northampton, of course, was trying to dismiss his defeat by Grove in the hard game of institutional politics as just so much fairy dust. There was nothing airy-fairy about the science that Grove championed though. With its emphasis on production, exchange and power – and its insistence on utility – it was a science forged in and for industry. That does not mean that Grove's science – or the science of the little societies sprouting across Victorian Wales – was only about use though. Its utility was an outgrowth of the effort to understand nature and humanity's place in it. It was about improvement, of self and of society. That is why Grove's (and science's) contribution to Welsh culture merits celebration.

Further reading:
Jack Morrell and Arnold Thackray, *Gentlemen of Science* (1981)

15

WALES AND THE GOLD RUSHES: THE VALIANT AND THE VARMINTS

Gethin Matthews

At first glance the idea of 19th-century emigrants as 'heroes' or 'villains' may seem a touch misplaced: after all, most Welsh emigrants in this period were, in today's terminology, economic migrants. These individuals were generally motivated by a desire for greater rewards for their labour and a better life for their families, and thus neither heroic deeds nor acts of villainy would have been on their immediate agenda. The principal ambition of, say, the tens of thousands of Welsh coal miners who moved to the coalfields of the USA in the late 1800s was to use their expertise to maximise their weekly pay-packet: they were therefore a very footloose and mobile breed, often moving from coal town to coal town according to the rise and decline of opportunities offered in the different coalfields. There was a specifically Welsh information network in operation in the American coalfields, allowing details of good prospects and job opportunities to be shared among the Welsh-American community: because of this network, Welsh coal miners would often end up being employed by Welsh mine bosses. Similarly, Welsh workers with experience in the iron or tinplate industries would use the information they received to travel to where the best prospects were to be found.

Although they had some clear differences, the mechanics of the 'Gold Rushes' were fundamentally similar to those of other forms of migration. As with the example of Welsh coalminers, the flow of information was vital in facilitating a Gold Rush so that the potential emigrants could decide whether and where to go (the difference here being that for gold-seekers, the answer to the question 'when to go' was always 'NOW!'). As with almost any other kind of migration, a crucial element in the process was chain migration – i.e. emigrants following a pathway that had already been trodden by a friend or relative. Sometimes it was the friend or relative who brought home the information personally, giving extra impetus to the emigration. One good example of this can be found in Merthyr in February 1859, when it was reported that twenty men had just left the town for the gold-fields of Australia, following the return from there of a local man with over £1,000 of gold in his pockets.

Yet, the idea of 'heroes' and 'villains' is worth considering in the context of the Gold Rushes, because there is often an allusion to these opposite archetypes in the contemporary literature about the gold-fields. Certain groups of men (and, given the lack of women in the stampedes, we *are* talking just about males) were presented in heroic terms; other groups were castigated as the bad guys in the narrative. These ideas were all tied up with the perceptions and norms of mid-Victorian society in Britain and America, and to be blunt about it, their prejudices. Thus the rugged individualist (white) gold-seeker who was venturing to unexplored lands to seek his fortune was inevitably cast as the leading man in the drama, whereas the Native American who sought to protect his territory and his community's way of life from the interlopers was presented as a bloodthirsty savage.

Within the Welsh context, there is a further subtlety to the way that the gold-seekers were presented. Those Welshmen who stayed true to the Welsh mid-Victorian virtues of sobriety and religiosity were reported favourably in the Welsh newspapers, many of which were associated with the Nonconformist chapels and their world-view (particularly the Welsh-language titles). Those Welshmen who organised Welsh societies or *eisteddfodau* in the gold-fields earned extra brownie points.

CHAPELS, TEMPERANCE AND PRODIGALS

It should not surprise anyone who has read about Wales in the 19th century to learn that there were numerous Welsh-language chapels and temperance societies in the gold-fields of California and Australia. (The only explicit mention of the Welsh in one magisterial study of the North American Gold Rushes notes that they ran the Temperance Association in the otherwise intemperate gold-rush town of North San Juan, California). There were Welsh services held in the California gold-fields from as early as 1849, and in the Victorian gold-fields there were at least twenty Welsh chapels established by 1865. Similarly, it should not surprise anyone who's ever seen a Western movie to learn that there were some Welshmen who strayed from the straight-and-narrow path, and who were to be seen more often in a saloon than in

North San Juan, California

a chapel. The tension which arose when Welsh gold-seekers were torn between these two worlds is often reflected in Welsh letters from the gold-fields. Thus William Jones wrote from Nevada City, California, to a Welsh-American religious journal in 1851 that 'many fall into temptation after coming to this country. Some were good members of the church at home but here they are wasters. Some, when at home, preached the gospel but here they feed among the pigs'. Many Welsh letters from this early part of the Gold Rush period, before the authorities managed to stamp a little authority on the mining settlements, are full of vivid details of the drunkenness, gambling and violence all around them, which is contrasted with the behaviour of the hard-working Welshman who is trying to make an honest living. Thus these Welshmen are presented as role-models of how the Welsh *should* behave, even in difficult circumstances.

The tension can also be seen in some obituaries. If the deceased was an upstanding individual who behaved himself then he would be praised, but on the other hand, the career of the Welshman who fell off the wagon could be used as a morality play to warn others against following the same course. Thus when Griffith Owen died in Lower Lake, California, in late 1873, having looked after his family and remained true to his Christian beliefs, he was mourned as a shining example of everything a Welsh man should be. However, when John Powell died in Hungry Creek, California, in 1879, 24 years after leaving his wife behind in Pennsylvania and 14 years after he had last written to her, the 'prodigal young Welshmen' who were 'wandering the Western States' were urged to 'remember your homes, and those who have remained faithful to you through the years'.

DAVID GRIER, HERO

The word '*arwr*' ('hero') is explicitly used to describe at least one Welshman who did the right thing having made his fortune in the gold-fields. David Grier, born in Llanarthne, Carmarthenshire, in 1822/3, was a builder in Aberdare before travelling across the Atlantic in the late 1850s, seeking his fortune. He made his way to British Columbia, where he was lucky enough to stake a claim on Williams Creek in 1861, which turned out to be one of the richest plots of land in the Cariboo gold-fields. Having made $15,000 that year, he sent some of the money home to his wife and family... and you can guess what the result of that was, amongst the young and adventurous men of

Williams Creek, Cariboo, showing the exact spot where David Grier struck gold in 1861

Aberdare. In the spring of 1862 there was a stampede from the town (as well as some nearby towns like Merthyr Tydfil and Beaufort) to the gold-fields of British Columbia. Most of the gold-seekers would be disappointed, as by the time they got to Cariboo too many men were searching for gold on the creeks, and, due to the laws of supply and demand, the cost of everyday necessities was sky-high. However, David Grier did his best to help his fellow-Welshmen, giving some jobs on his claim and lending money to others. Thus it is no surprise that in 1863 the newspaper *Seren Cymru* referred to Grier as '*arwr British Columbia*'.

There are further examples of David Grier being held in respect and promoted as a shining example of Welsh manhood. A poet named Thomas Gwallter Price, who had benefited from his generosity in the Cariboo gold-fields in 1862, wrote a song in praise of the rugged qualities of the Welsh gold-seekers, which is dedicated to David Grier. Published in the Aberdare weekly newspaper, *Y Gwladgarwr*, in early 1863, the song describes Grier as '*addfwyn, fwyn di-far, Gwiwbur deg o Aberdar*' – 'gentle, kind, slow to anger, worthy fair [man] of Aberdare'.

'COMPANY OF WELSH ADVENTURERS'

Other Welshmen were praised in the Welsh newspapers for their roles in supporting Welsh culture in the gold-fields. John Evans of Machynlleth led a party of 26 men from North Wales to the Cariboo gold-fields: the grandly named 'Company of Welsh Adventurers'. Evans (described in the papers as 'the right man for the job') ensured that his crew kept up the Welsh traditions, even as they toiled against the unpromising conditions to extract gold from the mud. The men held poetry competitions and, every Sabbath, Evans would ensure that it was a day of rest and prayer, with all work banned. However, this was to prove the undoing of the venture, as one Sunday in October 1863 the water wheel, which drove the pumps to keep their shaft free from water, iced up and by the time the workers attempted to salvage the situation on the Monday morning the mechanism was beyond repair.

Despite his poor track record in finding gold, John Evans became a respected member of the gold-field community and the *de facto* leader of the Welsh contingent. When the need for a building to hold the Welsh Sunday School became pressing, it was John Evans who successfully lobbied the authorities for the grant of land for the Welsh to build their 'Cambrian Hall' (opened in 1866); in the *eisteddfodau*, held every Christmas and St David's Day for the following five years, it was John Evans who presided over the meetings. The literary, musical and religious activities of the Cariboo Welsh were recorded in great detail in letters published in the Welsh newspapers in the late 1860s: two of the principal correspondents were John Evans and his son Taliesin. (Indeed Taliesin, who, like his father, failed to find very much gold, discovered his niche as a poet and writer, and was later to have an illustrious career as a newspaperman in San Francisco). As well as recording who sang what in the *eisteddfodau*, these reports had the implicit objective of portraying the Cariboo Welsh as worthy sons of the homeland. 'In the middle of the Babel-like mixture of languages that can be found here, the old language is spoken as boldly and plainly as between the dear rocks of Wild Wales' declared Taliesin Evans in 1867. 'In the midst of the hustle and bustle of the Cariboo gold-mines our country's institutions are not ignored'.

TALIESIN'S TRUMPET

As well as boosting the profile of the British Columbia Welsh back home in Wales, Taliesin was zealous in promoting their activities in the gold-field newspaper, the *Cariboo Sentinel*. So many articles flowed from his pen praising the cultural activities of the Welsh community that many of the non-Welsh gold-seekers must have scratched their heads and wondered 'Who are these guys?' As if to answer their question, Taliesin Evans wrote a long essay for the *Cariboo Sentinel* in January 1867 entitled 'The Welsh – Who Are They?', explaining that they were the most cultured people in the world: 'at the present time there is not a more enlightened or better informed nation on the face of the earth'.

The grave of John Evans of Machynlleth in Cariboo, British Columbia

The Welsh community in the Cariboo gold-fields did more than just talk and sing about their Welshness – they put their money where their collective mouths were. Following a mining disaster at Ferndale in the Rhondda in November 1867, in which 178 men and boys died, the Cariboo Welsh raised a collection at their St David's Day festivities in 1868 to support the widows and orphans. In addition, the Cariboo Welsh also organised a collection in late 1869 following the Avondale mining disaster in September 1869 in which 110 died. This fact is particularly interesting as, although most of the deceased miners were Welsh, the disaster happened in the Pennsylvania coalfield, demonstrating the transnationality of the Welsh community in Victorian times. Even though the gold-fields of the Pacific North-West were physically remote from Wales, both mentally and in their hearts the Welsh gold-seekers felt the connection with their homeland.

KNIVES AND CANDLESTICKS

Thus those who kept their Welshness and their morality in the challenging conditions of the gold-fields were presented as heroic in the newspapers back in Wales. On the other hand, there were some who transgressed the moral code of the time and who were thus presented as warnings of how not to behave. One such story was that of William Hughes, a gold-seeker in Howland Flat in Sierra County, California, who was in bed with a young lady in a house of ill repute in early 1863 when a jealous American miner named Thomas Lamarell burst into the room and started attacking him. Hughes grabbed a knife and stabbed the American in his breast and abdomen. Lamarell died twelve hours later, but the local sheriff accepted Hughes' plea of self-defence and so he was not prosecuted. However, one doubts that he would have been welcome in the local Welsh Sunday School after such shameful behaviour.

One of the saddest stories I have found from the Welsh community in the gold-fields is that of Noah Jones and David Jones. Noah was seeking gold in Chapperell Hill, Sierra County, California, having moved west with his wife and family from the Welsh community in the Pennsylvanian coalfields. There he made the fateful mistake of teaming up with David Jones, originally from Breconshire, and clearly one of life's losers. He already had a troublesome reputation in the gold-fields, where he was known as 'Dave killed the mule': he had lost so many fights that he had made a vow that he would not allow himself to be beaten again. On the morning of November 21, 1862, both Welshmen were working their claim together when a dispute arose about the best way to proceed; David picked up a heavy iron candlestick and stabbed Noah seven times in his chest. Noah lived for a few hours – long enough to state that he had not provoked the fight – but the jury accepted David's claim that Noah had struck him first, and so he was jailed for accidental manslaughter. He served three-and-a-half years in San Quentin for his crime. Noah left behind three children and a pregnant wife: I have no information of what became of them. The reporting of this incident in the newspapers shows that the Welsh were truly shocked that a fellow-countryman had sunk so low as to commit such an evil act.

Although the circumstances in the gold-rush towns were unusual, the story of the Welsh and their activities there does tell us a lot about how they saw themselves, and thus gives us an insight into the cultural mindset of Victorian Wales in general. It is clear that the Welsh gold-miners liked to portray themselves in a heroic light, particularly so for those who clung onto the Welsh traditions. The newspapers of the time were keen to print stories about the Welsh in such exotic locales, and were generally favourably inclined towards the gold-seekers, who were portrayed as nobly battling against adverse conditions in search of their fortune. The flipside of this was that when the men failed to do what was expected of them, they would instantly become the villains of the piece, and a stark reminder of the dangers of straying away from the Welsh moral code of the time.

Further reading:
Alan Conway, *The Welsh in America: Letters from the Immigrants* (1961)

16

CYCLISTS AS SPORTING HEROES... AND VILLAINS

Steven Thompson

Ask any Welsh person who their sporting hero is and you might hear the names of Gareth Edwards, Jonathan Davies or Shane Williams in answer. Those not sufficiently enamoured of the appeals of our 'national game' might reply with the names John Charles, Ryan Giggs or Aaron Ramsey, while still others might be tempted to offer Howard Winstone, Johnny Owen or Joe Calzaghe in any response. Very few Welsh people would name cyclists and yet, over a hundred years ago, a great many of our ancestors thrilled to the exploits of champion cyclists such Arthur Linton, his brothers Sam and Tom, and Jimmy Michael, all of them from South Wales.

Arthur Linton, champion cyclist

This is because, during the 1890s, Europe and North America witnessed a massive boom in the popularity of cycling, and various cyclists from South Wales became world famous sportsmen whose victories were heralded across the globe. They became massive celebrities whose lives and careers were followed avidly in local and national newspapers by legions of adoring fans. A long time before Nicole Cooke or Geraint Thomas won fame and celebrity for their exploits on two wheels, Welsh cyclists competed at the very highest level in the sport and became household names to a large swathe of the Welsh public.

THE 'CYCLING CRAZE' OF THE 1890s

The massive popularity of cycling in the 1890s had its origins in the technological developments that transformed the bicycle. The old 'penny farthings' were extremely difficult to master and many a rider suffered the indignity and pain of pitching head-first over the top of the machine and onto the ground. The development of the 'safety bicycle', with two wheels of equal size, pneumatic rubber tyres and a chain transmission, suddenly brought the bicycle within the purchasing capabilities of a much larger proportion of the population, and made cycling far easier and more pleasurable than it had ever been previously.

Cycling clubs sprang up across Britain as cyclists looked for opportunities to socialise while a-wheel, or wished to compete against one another in the races that clubs organised. Wales was no exception to this trend and clubs were formed across the country, especially in the more populated and affluent south of the country. For the most part, middle-class cyclists tended to join those clubs for which an outing in a rural location on the weekend was a social occasion and an opportunity to see local sights of interest, stop for tea and cakes, and enjoy the pleasures of conversation. Young, working-class men, on the other hand, preferred the dangers and excitement of racing, purchased the latest racing machines, and generally posed a nuisance to the inhabitants of towns and villages with their 'scorching' on public roads.

It is evident from contemporary newspaper reports that the racing scene in South Wales was intensely competitive. Large numbers of races were held in competitions in many of the larger towns and villages throughout this period and spectators thrilled to the dangers and excitements of high-speed races and the local heroes who brought glory to their home villages through their victories. Apart from the thrill of competition, young men were attracted by the prizes offered in these competitions, and the National Cycling Union considered South Wales to be a problematic region because of the cash payments and prizes that clashed with the amateur ethos it was trying to instil in races under its authority. For young, working-class men, used to physical strength being rewarded with monetary gain, amateurism had little appeal, and many racers turned professional rather than play the charade of amateurism.

CYCLING HEROES

Out of this competitive racing scene sprang a handful of riders whose ambitions and talents were greater than could be accommodated by this local racing environment. Some of the best Welsh cyclists travelled the globe to compete against the very best talents the cycling world could offer and earned massive fortunes, great fame and the undying adulation of adoring fans.

The first big star to emerge from the Welsh scene was Arthur Linton, from Aberaman, near Aberdare. He was born in Somerset but his family moved to Aberdare in the early 1870s and Linton was always glad to describe himself as a Welshman. Like so many other boys in the South Wales coalfield, Linton went to work underground at the age of twelve, in his case as a door-boy at the Treaman colliery, before later becoming a haulier at the age of 18. Such were his earnings that he was able to save some money and purchase his first bicycle, a penny farthing, before later adopting the safety bicycle as his racing machine.

Linton gained a number of victories in South Wales and across the border in 1890 and 1891, and came to be ranked as one of the 'crack' riders in Britain with his outstanding performance in the Cucu Cocoa Cup, an important 24-hour race in London, in July 1893. In that year, Linton decided to travel to Paris, the world centre of competitive track racing at that time, to compete in the big events that attracted crowds of more than 20,000 people. In a series of competitions at prestigious venues such as the Vélodrome d'Hiver, the Vélodrome Buffalo, and the Vélodrome de la Seine, and against the best racers that Europe could muster, Linton won a great many races, set time records at a variety of different distances, and earned fame and fortune as one of the elite athletes of his day.

Linton was a shy, taciturn man who offered little to those journalists who frequently sought interviews with him for their newspapers. And yet he was always held in the highest esteem by his peers, and was the object of a great deal of admiration and affection from the Welsh public, primarily perhaps as a result of his origins. Journalists frequently referred to Linton as 'the Welsh collier boy' and often insisted that he was 'a noble lad from such humble birth', and it is clear that, for their part, the Welsh public took to him precisely because he did emerge from a background that was so very familiar to the ones they had experienced. Cycling at this time, similar to boxing during much of the twentieth century, was often viewed by young, working-class men as a means to escape the poverty and limitations of their backgrounds and earn more money and a better lifestyle than could be achieved through the usual routes. The Welsh public gloried in the ascent of one of their own to such sporting success, fame and wealth.

The appeal of another Welsh hero, Jimmy Michael, also of Aberaman, was different but no less intense. A delivery boy for his grandmother's butcher's

Arthur Linton, surrounded by success

shop, Michael was also of relatively humble birth, but it was his character and riding style that most appealed to his fans. Often referred to by journalists as 'the Welsh midget' and 'the midget cyclist' because of his short stature, Michael was nevertheless able to turn the biggest gears on his bicycle to generate the most incredible speed in his races, speed that he was able to maintain for hours at a time without seemingly making a great deal of effort. His favourite trick was to race around the track at incredible speed while nonchalantly balancing a tooth-pick between his teeth and waving merrily to his many fans at track-side.

131

Michael followed Linton across to Paris and, due to his amazing prowess and incredible stamina, was an instant success with the Paris race-going fraternity, especially the female fans who were enamoured of his boyish good looks. He was equally successful in Cologne, Antwerp and other European cities, so much so that this former butcher's errand boy from Aberaman was the toast of sports and cycling journalists and avid cycling fans right across Britain. His status as a hero was nowhere greater than in South Wales, of course, where his many exploits were thought to raise the profile of Wales on the international sporting stage and bring glory to the nation.

This status was further enhanced when, later in the 1890s, Michael and his trainers decided that Europe was too small to contain his considerable talents and he travelled to America to compete in the lively race scene there. In a series of high-profile competitions against the best European and American racers, at such glamorous venues as Manhattan Beach and Madison Square Garden, New York, Michael achieved a series of high-profile victories that earned him 'dazzling stacks of American dollars', in the words of the *New York Times* correspondent.

ABERAMAN AND THE BIG APPLE

In one memorable series of races, Jimmy Michael competed against another Aberamanite, Tom Linton, brother of Arthur, in front of massive crowds and a band which welcomed the two gladiators into the arena with a rendition of 'Men of Harlech'. Michael's love of novelty saw him switch to horseracing in 1898 but with much less success; his tendency to describe the reins as 'handlebars' and the stirrups as 'pedals' was said to be disconcerting to the owners who entrusted their horses to him.

Unlike Linton, Michael was a garrulous character who loved to speak to the press, talk up his prospects in forthcoming competitions, in a way not dissimilar to boxers today, and create a spectacle wherever he went in order to attract as much attention as possible. Such was his fame and character that his personal life became the subject of a great deal of speculation and gossip when, in 1895, it was reported that he had married. Speculation in the newspapers and cycling press stated that he had married one of his adoring Paris fans, though the truth was rather more prosaic when it emerged that he had married Frances Lewis, the daughter of another Aberaman butcher. The marriage did not work out and Michael secured a divorce a short time later. He subsequently got into trouble for denying in newspaper interviews that he had ever been married, and solicitors acting for Frances Lewis were forced to refute these assertions in statements they issued to the newspapers.

The personal lives of sporting heroes, it seems, were of as much interest to newspapers and their readers at that time as they have been in more recent times.

CYCLING VILLAINS?

This bicycle racing scene also had less favourable aspects that perhaps leave these sporting heroes rather tarnished in appearance. One of these aspects was the tendency for large amounts of money to be waged on races, allied with suggestions that races were not always honestly raced to the best of the competitors' abilities. Cycling correspondents in South Wales were scathing in their criticisms of the deals done by competitors just before their races and the arrangements made as to which riders were going to be placed in which positions. In an era in which allegations of match-fixing, spot-betting and other nefarious activities are becoming commonplace, such practices in the 1890s perhaps demonstrate that cheating is as old as professional sport.

Furthermore, the appeal of some of the champion cyclists was lessened to some extent by the feeling that their success had taken them away from the communities that had nurtured and most cherished them. As they travelled to compete in the biggest British, European and American races, champion Welsh cyclists were less able to spend time in Wales and this was cause for regret for some who believed that Welsh races and the racing scene in Wales more generally would be enhanced by appearances from these stars. It was noted in 1896, for example, that the appearance of a Linton or a Michael would greatly add to the gate of a meet in Cardiff in that summer, but that the chances of this happening were slim.

Most significantly of all, few of the biggest Welsh cycling heroes lived to a ripe old age and there were suggestions at the time, and repeated since then by historians, that this was due to the substances that professional cyclists consumed to give them an edge in their racing. The *Tour de France* has been mired in drugs scandals during the last decade or so, and barely a week goes past without further suspicions about the world's top riders being aired in the media, and investigations being launched into the possibility of substance abuse in the sport. Substance abuse is as old as professional cycling, it seems, and Arthur Linton and Jimmy Michael have been suggested as the first victims of drug-use in the sport. Arthur Linton died in 1896, at the height of his powers, at the young age of 28. Most commentators attributed his death to exhaustion from his endeavours in the Bordeaux to Paris race six weeks previously, though the cause of death was given as typhoid fever,

Geraint Thomas

but some historians have speculated that he was under the influence of strychnine, trimethyl or heroin in that race, and that this was the real cause of death.

Similarly, Jimmy Michael died in 1904 at the age of 29, and claims were made at the time that this was due to the various substances with which he had been doped during his career. One journalist in South Wales argued that arsenic was the cause of his incredible strength and his eventual demise, and it was said that in the last few years of his career, as a result of the substances he had used, Michael was almost deaf, was slow-witted and veered across the track without warning during races, posing a risk to himself and his competitors.

Attention has come to be focused on the larger-than-life character 'Choppy' Warburton, a former powder-hall sprint champion from Lancashire, who had become a cycling trainer during the 1890s and had achieved great success with Linton, Michael and other champion racers. Warburton had been banned from tracks by the National Cyclists' Union in 1896 after being seen giving Michael a drink from a bottle just prior to a race, and it is perhaps significant that Warburton sued Michael for slander just a short time later, after Michael claimed that Warburton had tried to poison him. Arthur Linton and Jimmy Michael, therefore, have been viewed as the first in a sorry line of professional cyclists who have paid the highest price for their desire to succeed in this incredibly competitive and staggeringly arduous sport.

CONCLUSION

While the Welsh public rightly delights in the considerable achievements of Nicole Cooke and Geraint Thomas, most people are unaware of the long tradition of success in which these cyclists stand. Most people are not aware of the achievements of these Welsh cycling heroes of an earlier period who did so much to place Wales at the heart of these incredibly popular sporting activities in the late Victorian period and to delight

Nicole Cooke

Welsh fans with their considerable achievements. Such success was bought at a very high price, if contemporary and historical judgements are correct, and it behoves us in the 21st century to include the more villainous aspects of professional sport in our estimations of their heroic achievements. Perhaps a fitting tribute and memorial to these Welsh heroes of an earlier time would be for the Welsh Assembly to lobby the organisers of the *Tour de France* with the aim of holding one of the stages of the *Tour*, or even perhaps the start of the *Tour*, in Wales at some time in the future. This might again focus attention on these heroes of the Welsh sporting past and the price that is sometimes paid by sportsmen and women in their attempts to become sporting heroes.

Further reading:
Steven Thompson, '*Chwiw Feicio Cymru'r 1890au*', *Cof Cenedl* (2005), pp.133-65

17

WELSH RECRUITS IN THE FIRST WORLD WAR

Robin Barlow

Albert Perriman, a surveyor with a firm of architects in Newport, was typical of thousands of young Welshmen in August 1914. Surrounded by hoardings portraying Lord Kitchener with pointed finger, and a general air of patriotic support for the outbreak of war, he was 'stirred by the call'. Along with others from all walks of life – labourers, miners, clerks, teachers, farm workers – he enlisted at the local recruiting office, joining the 11th Battalion of the South Wales Borderers. After pledging to serve 'King and Country', Perriman was given (literally) the King's shilling and told to rendezvous at the Newport cattle market in two weeks' time. When he arrived, he was one of about a hundred others 'being pushed around like cattle by drovers masquerading as sergeants'.

The new recruits to the 11th Battalion then marched through the town 'to the cheers of the crowd lining the streets en route to the railway'. In his diary, Perriman remembers that 'we were being treated as national heroes'. And indeed 'heroes' they were – all the more so, because the promise of a glorious adventure to defeat the Germans by Christmas was so far from the reality that confronted the volunteers. Llewelyn Wyn Griffith described his first days in France, after leaving a wet quayside, on 'a grey ship on a grey sea': rain was beating against the trucks 'as we doddered through an unknown land to an unknown destination', standing in the mud of a station yard near St Omer. Griffith faced four days and nights of fatigue and stiff-limbed weariness, 'nights of little sleep and days of little rest'. It was to rain continuously for one hundred hours.

The volunteers would suffer danger, deprivation, mental and physical injury and illness with a forbearance, humour and fortitude hard to imagine in

15th Royal Welch Fusiliers at Fleurbaix, December 28, 1917

the pampered 21st century. Over 270,000 Welshmen (10% of the population) were to serve in the First World War, with one in nine of them losing their life.

CECIL PHILLIPS

A 'typical' recruit was Cecil Phillips from Llanelli, whose father was the postmaster there. Phillips had been training as a solicitor in London at the outbreak of war, but returned to Wales in the autumn of 1914 to join the 4th Battalion, Welsh Regiment, his local territorial battalion.

After training in Pembrokeshire, Tunbridge Wells, Scotland and Bedford – which hardly prepared him for anything that was to come his way – in July 1915, the battalion embarked on board ship for 'service overseas', with the only clue as to their destination being the issue of Eastern kit.

Though I have my faults and weaknesses I have always tried to be unselfish and I can honestly say I have never done anything very bad.

Cecil Phillips,
letter to his father

137

They were bound for the Gallipoli peninsula, where a campaign had begun (poorly) to try to deflect attention from the Western Front, and also knock Turkey out of the war. Phillips clearly thought his embarkation was a time for taking stock and settling his affairs. He wrote to his father giving him clear instructions on how to reclaim some overpaid income tax on his behalf, and in time-honoured fashion for departing sons, he also left a list of bills to be settled.

The original attacks on the Turkish forces on the Gallipoli Peninsula, in early August 1915, had proved disastrous. The terrain was rough and inhospitable, with steep and rocky cliffs leading up from the coastline where the allied troops were to land. All the advantages were with the defensive force. Phillips's 4th Battalion landed just south of Suvla Bay on August 9, totally unprepared for what was to come. Conditions for all the troops were appalling with unbearable heat, trenches like ovens and the constant presence of large, green 'corpse-flies'. Over 80% of the allied force was to succumb to dysenteric diarrhoea (the 'Gallipoli Gallop') at some time during the campaign, and a quarter of the troops had to be evacuated because of sickness. Phillips suffered just like the rest of his battalion. In a letter he described 'the frightful pains and sickness' and that he 'felt as weak as a cat'.

Of the 104 men from the 4th Welsh who died at Gallipoli, twelve died from sickness or disease. Hardly the heroic death that many of them might have imagined when volunteering at the height of patriotic fervour in the late summer and early autumn of 1914 – but heroes they were.

Cecil Phillips had gained a reputation in his battalion for being something of a 'mad jack'. Rather worryingly for his parents, he had written that he 'always walked about outside the trench, when the men would not show their noses out, just to give the men courage'. On August 14, 1915, Lt Cecil Phillips confirmed that his nickname was probably accurate when he rescued a fellow officer who was lying wounded, some seventy yards from the allied trenches, under heavy enemy fire. Phillips and a staff-sergeant from the 4th Welsh then repeated their heroic act a further three times, 'running a terrible gauntlet of fire'. For his 'great gallantry' Lt Phillips was awarded the Military Cross (MC) and promoted to captain, whilst Staff-Sergeant Grundy received the Distinguished Conduct Medal.

Their actions were brave, selfless and heroic – but no more or less so than countless others that took place throughout the Gallipoli campaign. 98 men from the 4th Welsh Battalion were buried on the peninsula and a further six were buried at sea. Phillips survived the war and resumed his career as a solicitor.

KEEP THE HOME FIRES BURNING

An unlikely hero of the First World War was David Ivor Davies, better known as Ivor Novello, born in Cardiff in 1893. However, it was certainly not his exploits in uniform which were to bring him acclaim. In June 1916, Novello had reported to the Crystal Palace training depot of the Royal Naval Air Service as a probationary flight sub-lieutenant. His skills as a pilot were soon found wanting; he managed to crash two planes and was swiftly moved to a desk job at the Air Ministry.

Two years earlier in 1914, Novello had composed the hugely popular and sentimental song 'Till the Boys Come Home' (better known as 'Keep the Home Fires Burning'), with words by the American poet Lena Ford. Sung by both servicemen at the front and families at home, the song's haunting chorus became an icon of the war:

> Keep the home fires burning
> While your hearts are yearning.
> Though your lads are far away,
> They dream of home.

Ivor Novello went on to achieve glittering success as an actor, film star, playwright and composer. During the Second World War, he also suffered a brief spell of villainy when he was imprisoned for four weeks in Wormwood Scrubs for misusing his Rolls Royce car during wartime petrol rationing.

THE WAR IN THE AIR

A noted character, flying ace and hero was James Ira Jones from St Clears, known universally (and unimaginatively) as 'Taffy'. He had transferred to the Royal Flying Corps in 1915 as a mechanic, then becoming an observer on flights over the German lines in northern France. In May 1917 he returned home to receive pilot training and was finally posted to 74 Squadron in early 1918. In just three months he was credited with shooting down 37 enemy aircraft ('victories') flying the SE5a. Jones had a reputation as a harum-scarum pilot and frequently crashed his planes on landing. In all, he somehow managed to survive 28 crashes.

Jones was one of the most highly decorated airmen of the First World War. He received the Distinguished Flying Cross (DFC) for destroying six enemy aircraft in eleven days, displaying 'great courage, skill and initiative'. He was then awarded the Military Medal, Military Cross and a Bar to his DFC. Finally, he received the Distinguished Service Order (DSO) in November 1918 for combining 'skilful tactics and marksmanship with high courage'. His citation described how, when on wireless interception duty, he followed a patrol of nine Fokker biplanes and managed to join their formation unobserved. Two Fokkers left the formation to attack an allied observation post. Taffy Jones pursued them and attacked the higher of the two which fell on its companion. Both planes became interlocked and fell to the ground in flames.

Although Jones had retired from the RAF in 1936, he was recalled to active service in the Second World War, aged 43. During the Battle of Britain, flying an unarmed Hawker Henley, he attacked a Junkers Ju 88 bomber armed only with a Very pistol, used to fire signal flares. Always a maverick (as befits a London Welsh scrum-half), Jones had a habit of attacking 'Huns' dangling from their parachutes, which apparently led to many arguments in the mess. Some officers 'of the Eton and Sandhurst type' thought it was 'unsportsmanlike' to do it. Jones said that as he had never been to a public school he 'was unhampered by such considerations of form'. He just pointed out that 'there was a bloody war on' and he intended to avenge his pals. Ironically, after surviving two world wars, Taffy Jones died after falling from a ladder at his home in Swansea, aged 65.

STICKY AND THE SOPWITH PUPS

Another singular airman was Tom Vicars, from Abermarlais Park in Carmarthenshire. He had joined the Rifle Brigade and was commissioned in December 1914. He was immediately sent out to the Western Front and was badly wounded in January 1915, resulting in the loss of a leg. Amazingly, in 1917 he then joined the Royal Flying Corps, serving in 66 Squadron, flying Sopwith Pups. He was promoted to Flight Commander in September 1917 and is credited with shooting down five enemy aircraft. In his squadron he was universally known as 'Sticky' because of his false leg. Apparently, whenever a mess party got too hectic, he would take off his wooden leg to avoid its being broken. Like many airmen of the First World War, he was not to be killed by enemy action. On December 5, 1917, he died in a flying accident in Italy.

FAMILY SACRIFICE

Many individual families were to make a heroic sacrifice in their support for the war. Robert Taunton Raikes from Treberfedd near Llangorse had six sons, five of whom were to serve in the First World War.

All five of the Raikes brothers were awarded the DSO for 'meritorious or distinguished service' and two brothers were awarded the MC. Only 8,981 DSOs were awarded throughout the war and 37,104 MCs. Geoffrey Raikes had joined the South Wales Borderers in 1903. He was awarded the DSO in 1916, followed by two Bars (in effect, two further DSOs) in 1917 and 1918.

He rose to the rank of Major General and was knighted in 1960. Perhaps, however, the greatest achievement of the Raikes brothers was that they all survived the war.

The Lowry family from Llandyfaelog was not so fortunate. They had three sons who served in the war, all of whom lost their life. Capt Auriol Lowry (awarded both the DSO and MC) and Lt Cyril Lowry died in northern France, whilst 2/Lt William Lowry died at Gallipoli. Their parents erected a ten-foot-high Celtic cross in the parish churchyard inscribed, 'To the Glory of God and in ever loving and proud memory of their three sons who gave their lives for King and Country'.

THE VICTORIA CROSS

The Victoria Cross is the highest and most prestigious award for valour in the face of the enemy. The list of those awarded the VC is a roll call of heroism. In total, 628 VCs were awarded in the First World War, 14 of them to Welshmen. The medals themselves are highly prized by collectors and can change hands for up to £400,000. Perhaps one of the most unusual awards was that to an undoubted hero, William Williams. Hailing from Amlwch on

The headquarters staff of the 15th Battalion (Carmarthenshire) Welsh Regiment (114th Infantry Brigade) after the capture of Pozieres, August 25, 1918

Anglesey, Williams was 23 years of age at the outbreak of war, serving in the Royal Naval Reserve. In 1917 he was aboard *HMS Pargust*, an ageing tramp steamer, but also a so-called Q-ship (or 'Mystery Ship'), named after their home port of Queenstown in Ireland. Williams had already been awarded the Distinguished Service Medal and Bar.

Britain had been desperate to find a counter-measure to the effectiveness of the German U-boats which were playing havoc with her sea lanes. Q-ships were heavily armed merchant ships, with concealed weaponry, usually carrying a cargo of balsa wood or cork to aid buoyancy if they were torpedoed. Despite their appearance they carried a full Royal Navy crew. Their aim was to use their apparent vulnerability to try to lure German U-boats into making a surface attack when they would then turn the tables and open fire. *HMS Pargust* was armed with a 4″ gun, two twelve pounders, two machine guns, torpedo tubes and depth charges.

On June 17, 1917, *HMS Pargust*, with William Williams on board, was patrolling an area of the sea south west of Ireland. The Q-ship was attacked by a German U-boat, *UC 29*, and struck by a torpedo at close range. One of the twelve pounder gun ports was blasted free from its mounting, which risked being seen and giving the game away to the enemy as to what sort of ship it was really dealing with. William Williams, with bravery and strength in equal measure, took the full weight of the gun covers on his back, preventing discovery of the weaponry. There was then a staged lifeboat evacuation from *HMS Pargust* (known as the 'Panic Party') – all part of the deception – which lured *UC29* within range. The gun crew then raised the White Ensign, a requirement of international law, and opened fire. The submarine was badly hit, split in two, blew up and sank. Capt. Ernst Rosenow and 22 of his crew were killed; there were two survivors.

Unusually, the Admiralty was unable to decide which members of the crew of *HMS Pargust* should be awarded the Victoria Cross, because all were deemed to have acted with equal valour. For the first time, under the conditions of the Royal Warrant for the award of the VC, it was decided that a ballot should be held by the crew for one officer and one enlisted man to receive the award. Following the vote, Seaman William Williams and Lt Ronald Stuart were awarded the Victoria Cross, although this was announced without fanfare or detail due to the secrecy surrounding the role of the Q-ships. Williams survived the war, returned to Anglesey and died in 1965. His VC is now held by the National Museum of Wales.

Welsh troops at the battle for Menin Road near Zonnebek, 1917

AFTERMATH

After the Armistice was signed in November 1918, Lloyd George, in a speech in Wolverhampton, asked the rhetorical question, 'What is our task?' His answer was, 'To make Britain a fit country for heroes to live in'. Of course, not all Welsh 'Tommies' were heroes – there were critics of the way some Welsh soldiers fought at the Battle of Mametz, for example. However, the vast majority defied Kitchener's comment that Welsh soldiers were 'wild and insubordinate', instead fighting with honour and bravery. One time resident of Swansea, Walter Savage Landor's description of those who fought in the Crimean War was equally relevant to the Welsh recruits:

> Hail, ye indomitable heroes, hail!
> Despite of all your generals ye prevail.

Further reading:
Hew Strachan, *The First World War: A New History* (2006)

18

WOMEN TEACHERS: THE UNSUNG HEROINES

Sian Rhiannon Williams

NOT ALL WELSH WOMEN WERE 'MAMS'

The Welsh 'mam' of the late 19th and early 20th century has become an iconic figure in our history. It's no wonder then that when we think of women's work in Wales, the images which immediately spring to mind are those of the miner's wife cleaning or washing, with baby in wraparound shawl and a crowd of children in tow, or the farmer's wife milking or butter-making. These working heroines serviced the Welsh economy, served their local communities and freed others to contribute to Welsh society more widely. Like other working women of this period, the majority of whom were domestic servants or seamstresses, their contribution deserves to be acknowledged, and, to some extent, it has been.

But not all women were mothers or domestic workers. There was another large group of female workers – schoolteachers. In elementary (later primary), intermediate and secondary schools, they taught generations of children, usually in very difficult circumstances, for lower salaries than those earned by their male colleagues. They often sacrificed in their personal lives for the sake of their jobs and their pupils. But how often do we remember those Miss Joneses and Miss Evanses who touched so many hearts and minds in the course of their professional lives? Our women teachers remain largely unknown and unrecorded in our history. These are our unsung heroines.

A 'VAST ARMY' OF WOMEN TEACHERS

In the twenty years between 1891 and 1911 the number of full-time teachers in Wales increased from 5,000 to over 14,000. By 1931, there were over 17,000 teachers; they accounted for almost a half of the professional

The students and staff of Glamorgan Training College, 1938

group of occupations as recorded in the census. Wales was no different to other European countries in that women outnumbered men in teaching and were mainly concentrated in lower status sectors in what was then a 'semi-professional' occupation. In the elementary schools (for 5–14 year olds) women comprised over 74% of the workforce in 1921. They completely dominated the Infant departments throughout the period, as today. Men dominated the more prestigious secondary sector. It was only during the First World War, when male teachers joined the army, that the number of women exceeded men in intermediate and secondary schools. Even so, up to 1939, on average, around 45% of Wales's secondary school teachers were women, and a very talented group of professionals they were too.

HARD WORK AND LOW PAY

Far from being an easy option, teaching in those days was a tough job, particularly in elementary schools. Classes of 60 or even 70 pupils were common, especially in urban areas. The work was demanding and stressful, and, as today, did not end when pupils went home. Parents did not hesitate to challenge teachers they disagreed with, sometimes with physical force, while some women teachers lived in fear of authoritarian headmasters.

We might think of teachers as high-earning professionals, but in the case of women teachers, we'd be mistaken. The very small proportion of university graduates who taught in the secondary sector were comparatively well paid, and most teachers became reasonably well off in retirement thanks to union campaigns for teachers' pensions. But the majority struggled to make ends meet.

Supplementary teachers, almost all of whom were female, only needed a clean bill of health and vaccination certificate to practise and earned as little as £20 a year in some areas in 1914. Other 'uncertificated' teachers (such as those who had originally been pupil teachers) again, mainly women, were also paid a less than professional rate, especially in rural districts. But whatever their status as regards qualifications and training, all women teachers earned less than their male colleagues for doing exactly the same work. The differential was usually between £10 and £20 a year in basic pay, and women were also paid smaller increments and bonuses. They had fewer promotion opportunities than men, and their pensions were lower.

It was rare that women teachers kept the whole of their own earnings. In Aneurin Bevan's family, where the girls were sent to training college, his sisters' pay when qualified supplemented the family income. Almost all the retired teachers I interviewed for my research said that a substantial portion of their income in the inter-war years went to support younger siblings through school or to help their widowed mothers or other relations. During the Depression of the 1930s, their financial contribution was crucial to the family economy. Many working-class teachers also had to repay training loans to their local education authority. As today, these were debts which took many years to clear.

The highest paid women were the headmistresses of intermediate and secondary schools, but because most of these schools in Wales were dual (twinned) rather than separate single-sex schools, the headmaster of the boys section was often in authority over the head of the girls' school. The first generation of headmistresses, such as Miss Margaret Cook of Aberdare, Miss Annie Dobell of Pontypool and Miss Catherine Davies of Llanelli were talented and inspirational leaders who believed in the power of education to enable girls to fulfil their potential and contribute fully to society.

SOUR-FACED SPINSTERS?

The popular image of women teachers in the inter-war years was that of the sour-faced, bespectacled and sexually repressed spinster. In Wales, as elsewhere, women teachers were ridiculed and derided in the popular press simply for being unmarried. Some parents, taken in by anti-spinster propaganda, felt that they were unsuitable role models for their daughters, having never raised a family of their own. At the same time, women were also considered unsuitable to teach boys of junior or secondary age. One slogan of the National Association of Schoolmasters, a single-sex male union, was 'Men teachers for boys!' It was a no-win situation.

Given that a marriage bar operated in most local authority areas and women had to resign their posts on marriage, it was no wonder that there were, as one of my respondents put it, 'many lovely unclaimed jewels in those days'. In order to retain their livelihood and make use of their talents and qualifications, they had to remain unmarried. Most of these singletons had no choice but to forgo marriage and children of their own for the sake of their jobs. Some did so gladly and celebrated their independent status and celibacy. Others were 'courting' for years on end, and a few, we know, were secretly married.

In the few areas where some married teachers were employed, such as Cardiganshire and Caernarfonshire, small rural schools were often staffed by a husband-and-wife team. In these cases the wife was under the authority of her husband, the headmaster, and usually taught the younger children and sewing to the girls. These women were particularly badly paid.

It was not easy to challenge the marriage bar since both legal and social norms upheld this discriminatory practice, but Wales' women teachers put up a fight. The first occasion was in 1908 when the Aberdare Urban District Council dismissed their certificated and very experienced married women teachers, five of whom were members of the National Union of Teachers (NUT). The matter caused much dissent; female members bravely stood up to their male colleagues, and were ready to strike to get the women reinstated.

Fresh-faced students not sour-faced spinsters!

But the NUT 'withdrew from the fight'. Similarly, their union refused to support the sixty married women who were dismissed by Rhondda Urban District Council in 1922. A high profile court case, 'Price v Rhondda', followed in May 1923. A large number of Rhondda teachers left the NUT and joined the strongly feminist union, the National Union of Women Teachers, over the issue.

It was not until the Second World War, when the men were called up for military service, that married women were again employed as teachers in Glamorganshire, Swansea, Cardiff, Carmarthenshire and elsewhere. Yet, their return was accepted only grudgingly, and, in most cases, was on a temporary basis. But the marriage bar was only one of several professional injustices which women teachers heroically opposed.

EQUAL PAY FOR EQUAL WORK

The best-known campaign by teachers for improved conditions of service was the fight for equal pay for women teachers. The Equal Pay League, formed in 1903, provided the basis of what became the NUWT, a separate union for women in teaching. These feminists broke away from the NUT in 1919–20 because the mixed union would not make equal pay and other women's issues priorities for action. After many years of tireless struggle, not least by members of Wales's two strongest NUWT branches, Swansea and Cardiff, equal pay was eventually won in 1961, but even then was only introduced incrementally!

NUWT: NOT DOORMATS!

Other courageous stands by the NUWT for a fair deal for women in teaching included opposing the marriage bar, the 'men teachers for boys' policy, and the financial cuts in education which led to combining single-sex schools under one (always male) headteacher, leading to the demotion of headmistresses. The outstanding personality of the Union was Swansea headteacher Emily Phipps, editor of *Woman Teacher*. Her two mottos were, 'She who would be free herself must strike the blow' and 'If you make yourself a doormat, do not be surprised if people tread on you!'

FIGHTING FOR A FAIRER FUTURE

Welsh women teachers need to be applauded for the part they played in campaigning for social and political change. Not only were our heroines at the forefront of efforts to improve teachers' pay and conditions, as in the Rhondda Teachers' Strike of 1919, in which women like Gwen Ray, Secretary of the Mid-Rhondda Teachers' Association, played a prominent part, they were also active in movements which they felt would ensure a better future for their pupils and their families.

Teachers were well represented among Wales's suffrage campaigners. Winning the vote for women was a key objective which women teachers of all political persuasion, and sectors of education supported. In Cardiff, for example, the headmistresses of both girls' secondary schools were leading members of Cardiff's thriving suffrage groups, and their staff and pupils were brave advocates of 'Votes for Women' and were unafraid of taking their protests to the streets. One of North Wales's leading suffragists, Charlotte Price White, was a former teacher, while Rachel Barrett, a very well-known suffragette in London, started her career as a teacher in Penarth.

Inspired by their professional struggles against gender inequality and seeing the social injustices their pupils faced, women teachers became involved in Liberal and

The frustrations and joys of the classroom

Socialist politics. In the South Wales valleys, where poverty affecting children was all too obvious, teachers such as Fannie Thomas of Pontycymer, a prominent member of the NUWT, and Rose Davies of Aberdare stood for election in local government and won in a period when women politicians were a rare breed. Rose Davies became the first woman member, alderman and Chairman of Glamorgan County Council, while Fannie Thomas sat on the Ogmore and Garw Urban District Council. They both worked tirelessly for social reform and for women's rights. Another inspired activist was Annie Powell of Rhondda who became a Communist local councillor and mayor.

WELFARE AND COMMUNITY

Issues such as maternity care, housing, juvenile unemployment and the establishment of nursery schools were causes which were particularly high on women teachers' political and social agendas. The welfare of pupils, both in and out of school, was a key concern of theirs. In addition to their role as class teachers, they also cared for the health and well-being of children. In times of distress, as during the Lock-outs of 1921 and 1926, they served meals and collected and distributed boots and clothes. They served as volunteer Red Cross workers, Air Raid Patrol wardens and billeting officers in wartime.

Teachers also often worked on weekends in local Sunday schools, taught in adult evening classes and helped run youth clubs. They supported and led cultural events and were pivotal to the social and cultural life of towns and villages throughout Wales. In those days, they were expected to live locally. In Glamorganshire for example, headteachers were contracted to reside within a two-mile radius of the school.

WELSH TEACHERS ABROAD

But not all teachers trained in Wales were able to get jobs locally. In the 1920s and 1930s a falling birth rate, economic crisis and harsh education cuts meant that Wales became over-supplied with teachers. Between the mid-1920s and mid-1940s, most newly qualified teachers (NQTs) had to move to England to obtain their first post. Young women were particularly badly affected and constituted the majority of out-migrants. Those who were eventually employed locally took longer than the men to find posts. In the training colleges of Swansea and Barry the girls would scan *The Schoolmaster* together searching for any job, anywhere, sharing the postage for application forms. 72% of Swansea's leavers crossed the border in 1943. They joined hundreds of teachers from Wales in London, the North of England and the Midlands, where they contributed greatly to educational and social life.

WARTIME DISMISSALS

The lack of jobs in Wales was the main reason for teachers moving, but others were forced out for a different reason. In 1940, Swansea Council dismissed teachers who refused to sign a 'Loyalty Oath' in support of the war. Miss Rosalind Bevan, a member of the local Peace Pledge Union, had to leave Wales and never returned.

Leaving home was often a traumatic experience, particularly in wartime. Former Swansea students had survived the Blitz there in 1941 only to face even greater dangers elsewhere. Among the barrage balloons and doodle bugs in Barking, Mary Jenkins and her friend spent three months sleeping in an air raid shelter, while Gwenllian Jones helped evacuate her school to Cheshire after months of teaching them in the same underground shelter.

150

As well as contributing to the teaching profession in England, Welsh women also made their mark as teachers internationally, particularly through the missionary movement, in India and elsewhere. These often exceptionally able and courageous women were motivated by evangelical and reforming zeal. Today we may be ambivalent about their complicity in imperialism, but in venturing abroad they broke the boundaries which restricted the world of women teachers in Wales itself.

SO, WHY HEROINES?

For their independence of thought, strength of character and moral courage; for the action they took to fight for equality and social reform; for their tenacity and steadfastness in the face of adversity; for their care for and interest in the education and welfare of their pupils and communities; for their personal sacrifices and for the way in which they inspired others, Wales's women teachers deserve the accolade 'heroines'. They may have been undervalued and oppressed in their own time, but they were never subservient. Through the hardship of the Depression and two world wars, they were absolutely indispensable to education and to society. It was not an easy time to have faith in the future, but that's what they had. It's time we sang their praises.

Further reading:
Sian Rhiannon Williams, 'Women Teachers and Gender Issues in Teaching in Wales, c. 1870–1950', *Welsh Journal of Education,* 13.2, 2005, pp. 68–83

19

GARETH JONES: A PIONEERING INVESTIGATIVE JOURNALIST

Toby Thacker

On August 17, 1930, a young Welsh journalist, Gareth Jones, wrote excitedly to his mother in Barry from the town of Stalino in Ukraine. At the top of his letter, he did not write 'Stalino', but 'Hughesovka', underlining the word four times. This was what the town was called when Jones's mother had worked there as tutor to the grandchildren of John Hughes, the engineer from Merthyr Tydfil engaged by Tsar Alexander II in the 1870s to develop Russia's iron industry. Gareth Jones did not stay in Hughesovska – as it was usually spelt – for more than a few hours though, for reasons which he could only disclose when he arrived in Germany some days later. The whole day he was in Hughesovska on his 'pilgrimage', he had only been able to get a single bread roll to eat. Now away from Soviet eyes, he felt free to write truthfully about what he had seen while travelling around Russia and Ukraine, concluding that 'Russia is in a <u>very bad</u> state'.

Jones returned to Russia in August 1931, in the company of Jack Heinz II, the heir to the '57 varieties' empire, and again in March 1933. On this last visit, Jones disregarded the recent ban on journalists leaving Moscow, and walked on his own for forty miles through the once fertile Ukrainian farmlands, scribbling his impressions down, as ever on his travels, in a small notebook. In every village and collective farm he walked through, his horrified earlier visions of Soviet misrule were confirmed, and he realised that he was witnessing a famine of biblical proportions. As soon as Jones got back to Germany at the end of March, his reports of the famine in Ukraine were published in leading newspapers in

... rotten; no food, only bread, oppression, injustice, misery among the workers, and <u>90%</u> discontented, I saw some very bad things, which make me wild. [...] The winter is going to be one of great suffering there and starvation. The government is the most <u>brutal</u> in the world.

Gareth Jones's description of Russia in 1930

Britain, in Germany, and in the USA. The *Manchester Guardian* declared on March 30, 1933: 'Russia to-day is in the grip of famine, which is proving as disastrous as the catastrophe of 1921, when millions died.' The *London Evening Standard* carried an article signed by Jones the next day, entitled 'Famine Rules Russia'.

Jones's account, based on eye-witness testimony, followed hard on the heels of similar reports by the former Communist sympathiser Malcolm Muggeridge; together they generated enormous controversy. The Soviet Union was being held up at this time as the model for a new civilisation, a 'paradise' where Stalinist Communism was bringing the blessings of technology and agricultural collectivisation to end for ever

Gareth Jones, getting to know the locals on the ground

the iniquities of the class system. From all sides, Jones was denounced: by Soviet officials, by Communist sympathisers in the West, and by journalists, some of them in the pay of the Soviet Union. In the *New York Times*, Walter Duranty dismissed his news as 'a scare story'. Although Jones responded vigorously and courageously to his opponents, his voice was all but drowned out by the propaganda apparatus of Stalin, and his supporters in the West. Over the next 15 years, Sidney and Beatrice Webb, those luminaries of

the British Labour movement, although they did not refer to Jones by name, insisted in various editions of their huge work *Soviet Communism: A New Civilization* that there had been only a 'partial failure of crops' in Ukraine, and that 'there was, at no time, a total lack of bread', contrary to the statements made 'by persons hostile to Communism'.

Gareth Jones in investigative mood in China

153

THE BACKGROUND: BARRY, ABERYSTWYTH, AND CAMBRIDGE

Who was this upright and intrepid reporter? Gareth Jones was born in Barry in 1905; his mother, Annie Gwen, was a prominent suffragist; his father, Edgar, was headmaster of Barry County School, which Gareth attended. From there Gareth, whose first language was Welsh, went on to study modern European languages at university in Aberystwyth, and in Strasbourg. Quickly demonstrating remarkable ability in German and French, Gareth went on to Trinity College Cambridge to study Russian. From the time he left school, Gareth was an indefatigable traveller, and he took every opportunity to go overseas,

cultivating friends and contacts in France, Germany, Italy and Poland which were to be useful to him later. He was lucky – graduating, like today's students, when unemployment was rising steeply – to be taken on in 1930 as an adviser to David Lloyd George, then Father of the House of Commons, and still very much involved in international affairs. Lloyd George was struck by Gareth's obvious intelligence and energy, and undoubtedly took a shine to this young man from Barry. He initially paid Gareth £500 a year to help him with secretarial duties, notably with the compilation of his *War Memoirs*, published in 1933, but also recognised and encouraged Gareth's potential as a reporter on foreign affairs. This was the break Gareth needed. With letters of introduction from the former Prime Minister he was able to gain access in the next few years to people of influence, and, no less importantly, he had the money to travel to far flung places.

Lloyd George was not alone in spotting Gareth's talent. While in New York in 1931, he was taken on as a reporter by the publicist Ivy Lee, and it was through him that Gareth was introduced to Jack Heinz, his travelling companion to the Soviet Union in 1931.

David Lloyd George, an early spotter of Gareth Jones's talent

Between 1930 and 1933, Gareth developed his unique style as a roving reporter. He

154

travelled constantly, crossing seas and continents, and always recorded his impressions in his notebooks, and in letters back home to 'Dear All' in Barry. These notebooks and letters, today in the National Library of Wales in Gareth's university town of Aberystwyth, provided the raw material for his journalism. The many articles which Gareth published at this time, above all in the *Western Daily Mail and South Wales News*, typically paraphrased whole passages from his notebooks. Everywhere he travelled, Gareth sought out politicians, diplomats, industrialists, and people of influence. He had an uncanny sense of where history was being made, and of who was making it, and the magic name of Lloyd George helped to open doors.

JONES'S CV OF INTERVIEWS

The list of the great, the good, and the not so good interviewed by Gareth Jones in the early 1930s is extraordinary, and includes the Polish Foreign Minister Józef Beck, the Irish President Eamonn de Valera, the German Foreign Minister Julius Curtius and the then Mayor of Cologne Konrad Adenauer, the Soviet Foreign Minister Litvinov, the Soviet Ambassador to London, Ivan Maisky, and Lenin's widow, Nadezhda Krupskaya. Travelling through America in 1934 and 1935, Jones managed to interview the novelist Upton Sinclair ('charming, but meek and mild') and the architect Frank Lloyd Wright, a man very conscious of his Welsh heritage. Jones had already interviewed the newspaper tycoon Randolph Hearst at St Donat's Castle in Wales, and secured an invite to the Hearst ranch at San Simeon in California.

'THE MOST THRILLING THING IN MY LIFE, ABSOLUTELY PRIMITIVE': JONES IN NAZI GERMANY

In May 1932 Lloyd George, who grilled Jones after every foreign excursion, asked him to travel again to Germany to investigate a phenomenon which was causing concern around Europe, the rise of Nazism. Gareth excitedly wrote to his parents from the Lion Hotel in Cricieth: 'Ll. G. is extremely anxious for me to go and see Hitler as soon as possible. So I may rush off to Germany as soon as an interview can be arranged! Won't that be fine!' In fact it was not until January 1933 that Jones left Southampton for Germany on the liner SS *Bremen*, and although he was not able to interview Hitler, who was appointed Chancellor on January 30, he was able to pull off a remarkable scoop. He was allowed to travel with Hitler on his chartered aircraft to an election rally in Frankfurt, and after this, to interview Hitler's closest confidant, Joseph Goebbels. Although Jones's notes of this meeting suggest that he was asking all the questions, this was clearly not the case. Goebbels was also an inveterate scribbler, and in his own diary he recorded that he had had a 'long chat with Lloyd George's secretary', 'a clever young man' who had told him 'terrible things about the Soviet Union'. In a series of articles published in the

155

Western Daily Mail, Gareth recorded his impressions of Germany in the heady grip of what the Nazis called 'the national revolution', warning in June 1933 that there was 'a profound danger to the peace of Europe in years to come'.

GOEBBELS OF GLAMORGAN, HITLER OF CRICIETH

Whilst Gareth Jones likened Goebbels to 'the dark, small, narrow-headed Welsh type which is so often found in the Glamorgan valleys', he compared Hitler with Lloyd George: 'Take away the wit, take away the intellectual play, the gift of colour, the literary and Biblical allusions of the Welsh statesman. Add a louder voice, less varied in tone, a more unbroken stretch of emotional appeal, more demagogy, and you have Hitler.'

'THE JAPANESE ARE HEADING FOR A WAR'

Gareth Jones was not obsessed with what would today be called celebrities, and he never forgot his own roots. On his travels he always talked with ordinary people, recording their observations on everyday life, their jokes, and their comments on their rulers. His notebooks show that he carefully recorded the things our MPs have today allegedly lost touch with, like the price of a loaf of bread, of potatoes, and of coal. Amongst details of conversations with diplomats and politicians, there are sections in his notebooks with headings like 'man in train', 'tobacconist', 'waiter', and 'barber'. He took great pleasure in meeting people from Wales in far-flung places, and in seeing how Welsh culture, hospitality, and humour were alive around the world. In his letters home he enthusiastically reported meeting compatriots. So in a letter from Hollywood in December 1934, we read: 'One of the porters is from Newport!' Arriving in Yokohama, he described how he was greeted with '*Shwd y'chi heddiw*?' ('How are you today'), by the Consul, a 'Mr W. J. Davies of Carmarthen'.

After reporting on the famine in Ukraine, Jones was undoubtedly disillusioned by the campaign of disinformation mounted against him. He was personally banned from further visits to the Soviet Union by Litvinov. It did not help that Lloyd George was (from a safe distance) an admirer of Stalin. After publishing a set of articles on Welsh rural life based on a walking tour, Jones turned his restless attention back to the New World, and beyond that to the Pacific. Travelling through the United States at the invitation of Randolph Hearst, giving lectures and broadcasts, he arranged an extensive tour of the Far East, to take him to Japan, and eventually to another hot spot of conflict, the region of Inner Mongolia seized by Japan in 1931 and re-named Manchukuo. The letters back to Wales, written from ships and hotel rooms, and finally from a yurt, track his progress: from Honolulu in January 1935 to Tokyo in February; on to the Dutch East Indies – where he visited an opium factory – to Singapore, Bangkok, Saigon, Shanghai, and in July to Peking. As ever, Jones revelled in the opportunities to learn about new cultures and languages, and to meet people of all kinds. Earnestly he discussed the issues of the day with fellow journalists, with European expatriates, and with local people, asking above all whether Japanese expansionism would lead to war with the USA and with the European colonial powers. In Japan he interviewed senior military figures, and the former Ambassador to the League of Nations, Yosuke Matsuoka.

After leaving Peking in July 1935, Jones was getting further and further off the beaten track and his last letters describe increasing practical difficulties as he pressed on towards Manchukuo accompanied by a German friend, Herbert Müller. He tried to reassure his parents, writing that Inner Mongolia 'is safe – no bandits'. In August 1935, Jones and Müller were indeed captured by bandits; Müller was released, but Jones was killed. The precise circumstances of his death have never been clarified, but there were suspicions, never confirmed, that the Japanese or the Soviet secret police were responsible. The latter was certainly the view of two obituaries to Jones published in Germany by friends of his there. Other published notices of his death hinted at the involvement of the Japanese.

'MR GARETH JONES KNEW TOO MUCH OF WHAT WAS GOING ON'

In Britain, and in Wales, the unfulfilled potential of a brilliant journalistic talent was particularly lamented. But in a country preoccupied by darkening war clouds and the threat from Hitler's Germany, events moved on, and Gareth Jones's brief career was soon largely forgotten. The importance of his journalism has only been fully recognised since the collapse of the Soviet Union in the 1990s. To Ukrainians around the world supporting their country's aspirations to break free from Soviet domination, Jones has become a national hero. Largely through the untiring work of his relatives, Jones's pioneering role in publicising the Ukrainian famine has become more widely known, and he has been the subject of books, films, and an exhibition held at the United Nations in New York in November 2009. He is today at the centre of the debate on whether the Ukrainian famine was a natural disaster, or a consciously-willed genocide. In 2006 a plaque celebrating his achievements – written, appropriately, in

> He had the almost unfailing knack of getting at things that mattered.
>
> Lloyd George's personal tribute to Jones, quoted in the *London Evening Standard*

English, Welsh, and Ukrainian – was unveiled in the Quadrangle of the Old College at Aberystwyth University.

How should we assess Gareth Jones's journalism today? Much of his reporting was anecdotal rather than analytical, and as he made only brief visits to different countries, he was not able to present a sustained investigation of one country, like his contemporary William Shirer. He did though have an extraordinary sense of what was most important in the world around him, and managed to penetrate to the heart of the great ideological controversies of his time. There is a remarkable prescience to much of his reporting. Although Jones was not alone in predicting that Hitler's foreign policy would lead to war, he saw, as few other contemporaries did, that hatred of the Jews was a central part of Nazism, and not something adopted for opportunistic or tactical reasons. And, for a brief period, Gareth Jones's reporting meant that his readers in Wales were among the best informed in the world. They heard from him for example, in February 1933, that Goebbels would soon be the head of a propaganda ministry, two weeks before this was actually announced in Berlin. Above all, while Gareth Jones was fiercely proud of his Welsh linguistic and cultural heritage, he recognised that Wales was part of a larger world, and he did his best to bring knowledge and understanding of that wider world back to Wales.

Further Reading:

There is no single easily available book, but anyone interested in Gareth Jones should visit the excellent website www.garethjones.org which has many of his published articles as well as much interesting biographical material about him.

20

SOUTH WALES MINERS: THE MYTHS AND THE MILITANTS

Ben Curtis

The South Wales miners were one of the most important groups of workers in Britain in the twentieth century. In the early years of the century, when the coal industry was at its height, South Wales was the largest and most important coalfield in Britain. At this time, the South Wales miners and their union, the South Wales Miners' Federation (SWMF, or 'the Fed'), acquired a reputation as socialist radicals. In 1917 the Fed's constitution was re-written to include the abolition of capitalism amongst its objectives!

The South Wales Miners' Federation (and its successor, the NUM South Wales Area) was much more than a union, in many respects. In addition to representing its members, it played a broader role within coalfield society. Its Workmen's Institutes spread throughout the valleys, ran leisure and cultural events, established medical schemes and built libraries for their members. Although coal's importance diminished as the twentieth century progressed, the South Wales miners and their industry remained an important part of the society and economy of Wales until the 1980s. In the epic industrial disputes of that decade, no other group of workers contested Thatcherism more obviously than the South Wales miners. Their struggle against the policies of the Heath and Thatcher governments reflected a recurrent theme in the miners' history: their ready involvement in the life of valleys communities and their willingness to fight for social justice.

MORE THAN A TRADE UNION

In 1945, the SWMF became the South Wales Area of the newly-formed National Union of Mineworkers (NUM). The NUM South Wales Area retained the Fed's substantial socio-political presence and took an active interest in its members' well-being. It maintained the recreational, cultural and educational traditions of the valleys miners' institutes, which reached their zenith in the 1950s. The Tredegar Workmen's Institute, with its silver band, operatic and choral societies, cinema and impressive library, was by no means untypical. The South Wales NUM continued the SWMF's medical care programme and expanded its education system in 1956. The decline of the coal industry in the 1960s dealt a severe blow to many valleys communities. In addition to the economic impact, a colliery closure also meant the loss of the community leadership, cohesion and local institutions provided by its NUM lodge. Nevertheless, the lodges at the pits which remained continued to play an important role within the lives of their members.

The historical contribution of the South Wales miners to their communities was immense, both in terms of physical infrastructure (welfare halls,

'The bond between miners and local communities ...' Aberfan, 1966

libraries, sporting facilities) and traditions of culture and self-education. This participation in community life remained a feature of the miners right down to the late twentieth century. This could take various forms: for example, organising annual pantomime outings for miners' children, delivering Christmas hampers to retired members, paying regular contributions to local charities and organisations, or organising brass bands and rugby and football teams within the community, amongst other social activities.

The strength of the bond between miners and local communities in the South Wales coalfield could also be seen in times of disaster and crisis. On October 21, 1966, a hillside waste tip slid and engulfed part of the village of Aberfan, killing 111 children and 33 adults. Around 1,000 miners from nearby Merthyr Vale colliery arrived to lead the rescue effort. They were joined afterwards by the emergency services and men from collieries throughout the region, in a massive rescue operation which lasted several days. Thousands of miners subsequently attended the funeral service for the victims of the disaster.

This affinity of lodge and community meant that the Area regularly took a central role in campaigns on local issues not directly connected to the coal industry. The 1970s saw an increase in the Welsh miners' participation in these struggles: for example, supporting Merthyr Borough Council's opposition to school milk cuts, support for opposition to the Housing Finance Act by Bedwas and Machen Urban District Council, protests against the siting of gas storage tanks in Hirwaun, and the campaign against the closure of DHSS buildings in the Garw Valley. Less dramatic – but no less indicative of this close relationship – was the Area's criticism of the inadequacies of arrangements to enable miners to buy their NCB-owned homes, and the call at its 1973 conference for a major house-building programme to alleviate the shortage of affordable accommodation.

The year 1973 saw the opening of the South Wales Miners' Library. Established as a part of University College Swansea and continuing to operate to the present day, the Library's role was to promote adult education and also to provide an archive for a wealth of lodge records and books from institute libraries which would otherwise have been lost. As the NUM's newspaper *The Miner* reported at the time, 'The library is intended to help forge closer links between the University and the South Wales community as well as being a testimony to a generation of miners fervently committed to improving the standards of working class education'.

As real democrats we have a responsibility to stop an oppressive Government just as in the early 1930s the German trade unions had a responsibility to prevent the spread of Nazism ... We have a social responsibility to take extra-Parliamentary action against Mrs Thatcher's Government.

Emlyn Williams (South Wales NUM President, 1974–85) at the 1981 Area Conference

THE CONSCIENCE OF THE TRADE UNION MOVEMENT

An important aspect of the political outlook of the South Wales NUM was its internationalism. One example of this was the South Wales miners' longstanding friendship with Paul Robeson, the American singer on whose behalf they campaigned successfully when his passport was withdrawn during the USA's McCarthyite period in the 1950s. Opposition to American military involvement in Vietnam was the main focus of the international concerns of the South Wales miners in the later 1960s. Throughout this period, unanimously-carried resolutions calling for an end to the war were a recurrent feature of Area conferences and May Day rallies. In addition to this, South Wales miners were active in lobbying parliament and supporting anti-war conferences. They also campaigned for an end to apartheid in South Africa, as well as offering aid to opponents of the military dictatorships in Spain and Greece.

As trade unionists, the South Wales miners knew the importance of solidarity with other groups of workers. Throughout the second half of the twentieth century, the South Wales NUM supported strike action by nurses, teachers, car workers and steelworkers, to name but a few groups. In the early

Margaret Thatcher, the Prime Minister who tackled the NUM

1970s, the South Wales miners, alongside the rest of the trade union movement, campaigned against the Heath government's Industrial Relations Act. The election of the Thatcher government in 1979 increased the likelihood of further clashes, as it was determined to both cut public expenditure and introduce anti-union legislation.

> I won't call it a strike. I would call it a demonstration for existence. The miners in South Wales are saying 'we are not going to accept the dereliction of our mining valleys, we are not allowing our children to go immediately from school to the dole queue. It is time we fought'.
>
> Emlyn Williams at the outset of a strike by the South Wales miners in February 1981 against the pit closure programme

THE FIGHT TO DEFEND MINING COMMUNITIES

The South Wales miners knew that coal was the lifeblood of the valleys mining communities to which it had given birth. Following the nationalisation of the coal industry in 1947, the National Coal Board (NCB) remained the biggest employer in South Wales for much of the post-war period. There were 88,000 mineworkers on its books in 1962, 14% of the total labour force. As late as 1984, there were still around 20,000 miners in South Wales. During the struggles against pit closures in the 1980s, the miners adopted the slogan 'Cau pwll, lladd cymuned' and – in English – 'Close a pit, kill a community'. They knew what was at stake and were determined to defend it.

With the advent of coal nationalisation in 1947, the South Wales miners hoped that the hardships they had faced in the 1920s and 1930s were behind them. For the first few years this did indeed seem to be the case. Coal was in great demand: annual output in South Wales attained a post-war maximum of 23 million tonnes between 1950 and 1955. This situation did not last. In the late 1950s the seemingly unlimited demand for coal ceased, due to increasing use of oil and gas. South Wales was affected severely: output fell from 23 million tonnes in 1957 to 12.8 million tonnes by 1969, with manpower levels falling from 104,600 to 42,600. There was sporadic opposition to pit closures throughout these years, although it never became a concerted campaign of action.

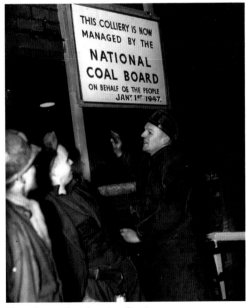

The advent of coal nationalisation

163

Pickets and police at Port Talbot, 1984

Pit closures effectively ceased in the 1970s. After a few years of relative stability however, the 1980s saw the reappearance of a major closure programme. In February 1981 the NCB announced the closure of 23 pits, including five in South Wales. The Welsh miners led the resistance, encouraging stoppages elsewhere and raising the prospect of a national strike. The government backed down, although this was not a significant defeat and merely strengthened Thatcher's resolve to tackle the NUM later. Coal stocks were increased from 37 million to 57 million tonnes between 1981 and 1984, so as to withstand any future strike. In the meantime closures continued piecemeal. In February 1983, the proposed closure of Blaengwrach and Lewis Merthyr collieries prompted a stay-down strike at Lewis Merthyr. By the end of the month all the South Wales miners were on strike. Thousands of the Area's activists lobbied every pit in Britain, to persuade them to join their struggle – but in March 1983 a national ballot decisively rejected industrial action.

The miners' strike of 1984–85 was a landmark in 20th-century British domestic politics. The strike was triggered on March 6, 1984, when the NCB announced the closure of Cortonwood colliery in Yorkshire and Polmaise colliery in Scotland. Two days later, the NUM leadership endorsed the stoppages already underway in Yorkshire and Scotland and urged the other coalfields to support them. After a slow start, South Wales was soon completely on strike and was the most solid Area for the entire dispute. This turnaround was rooted in the Area's traditional commitment to union solidarity. By August 1984, only *one* miner had returned to work in the whole coalfield, whilst 21 of the 26 British pits still completely free of strikebreakers in mid-December 1984 were to be found amongst the 28 South Wales collieries.

South Wales was probably the most active NUM Area in picketing strategic targets, in addition to its activities in the coalfields. By the end of March 1984, the Area's miners were picketing or monitoring 26 power stations (as far afield as Lancaster and Essex) and were manning regional fund-raising centres at Birmingham, Swindon, Southampton, Worcester, Crewe and Devon.

The strike's most notorious incident was the 'Battle of Orgreave' on June 18, 1984. Thousands of miners (including thirty coach-loads from South Wales) converged on the Orgreave coke-works, where they were met by 8,000 police equipped with riot gear, dogs and horses. During the ensuing struggle, riot police staged medieval-style mounted charges against the miners and also used dogs to maul them. As one miner later commented, the police 'done everything bar turn guns on us'. The NUM's defeat at Orgreave was a key turning point in the dispute.

Of all the British coalfields, support for the strike remained strongest in South Wales. On August 1, 1984, all of the South Wales NUM bank accounts, including its food funds and those of some support groups, were frozen. The Area's survival through another seven months of struggle was due to the popular support for the strike in the valleys and the self-discipline of mining communities there. In mid-November 1984, 99.6% of the South Wales miners were still on strike (the highest percentage of any coalfield), compared with the national average of 73.7%.

From January 1985 onwards the pressure of sustaining the strike was placing a major strain on the South Wales miners, but as late as February 14, 98% of them were still on strike. After the final breakdown of negotiations in late February 1985, though, there had been a significant return to work: 5% in South Wales but around 50% nationally. In response to these developments in the other coalfields, on March 1, 1985, a South Wales Area Conference decided to call for an immediate national return to work. Two days later, a National Delegate Conference brought the strike to an end. This decision was an extremely controversial one for the South Wales miners. Nevertheless, the return to work on March 5 provided one of the iconic images of the strike: at Maerdy colliery, miners marched back to the pit en masse, scenes which were broadcast all over the world. United and defiant, the Maerdy miners epitomised why the South Wales miners had remained in the forefront of the NUM's fight to save jobs and mining communities.

Subsequent history has proved that the miners' fears were justified. Research published in 2005 by Sheffield

History will record that the British miner decided on a strategy of industrial action because he could not accept that the role of families was to go to unemployment exchanges... This has been... a strike on behalf of every man, woman and child in the United Kingdom... The miners have said, we are standing up to be counted.

Emlyn Williams, speaking in January 1985, on the reasons for the 1984–85 strike

Emlyn Williams, South Wales NUM
President at the time of the Miners' Strike

Hallam University showed that South Wales was the coalfield worst hit by the collapse of the industry. Twenty years after the end of the 1984–85 strike, only 19% of the jobs lost by the coal industry in South Wales had ever been replaced by work in other industries.

FAMOUS MINERS' LEADERS

The NUM South Wales Area (and its predecessor, the SWMF) produced several exceptional leaders. Each one of these could easily have been a subject of their own article in this book!

For the post-war period the first of these is Arthur Horner, a lifelong Communist from the Rhondda, who rose through the ranks to become President of the 'Fed'. He was known as 'Little Arthur' but was a real giant of the British trade union movement. He played an important role in the formation of the NUM in 1945, becoming its first General Secretary. In this role, he was closely involved in the negotiations that shaped the Coal Industry Nationalisation Bill. Many of the improved circumstances in the post-1947 industry came from the 1946 Miners' Charter, which was drafted by Horner.

After Horner, another great figure was Will Paynter. Like Horner, he was also a Rhondda Communist. Also like Horner, he became President of the South Wales miners, before being elected as national General Secretary of the NUM (from 1959 to 1968). In this role, he succeeded in introducing the National Power Loading Agreement (NPLA) in 1966. The NPLA was a big step forward, introducing wage equality between all the different coalfields, which did a great deal to increase the unity of miners across Britain.

Within the South Wales coalfield, two other famous figures were Dai Dan Evans (South Wales NUM General Secretary, 1958–1963) and Dai Francis (South Wales NUM General Secretary, 1963–1976). Both were Welsh-speaking Communists from the west of the coalfield. In addition to their qualities as leaders, both men cared deeply about the culture and history of the South Wales coalfield. Both played important roles in establishing the annual Miners' Eisteddfod (in 1947) and Miners' Gala (in 1953). Dai Francis was even elected to the Gorsedd of Bards at the National Eisteddfod in 1974, in recognition of his long-standing work in support of Welsh culture.

Further reading:

Hywel Francis and David Smith, *The Fed: A History of the South Wales Miners in the Twentieth Century* (1980)

21

COALITION POLITICS: THE HEROES AND VILLAINS OF THE WELSH LIBERAL PARTY

Russell Deacon

After a gap of 65 years the Welsh Liberal Democrats went back into a coalition government in Westminster in 2010. A decade earlier they had done the same in Wales but that time with the Labour Party. Coalition governments have over the last three centuries had a profound effect on the history of the Welsh Liberals. Although history is still unfolding in respect of the current Liberal-Conservative government, we can see what it tells us about the previous coalition governments and their impact on Liberal fortunes and how it has created both Liberal heroes and villains.

Since the formation of the Welsh National Council on October 7, 1887, the Welsh Liberals have been involved in many different coalitions. Indeed no other existing political party has been so shaped by coalition government. Throughout their existence the choice as to whether to form a coalition government with the Conservatives (Tories) or the Labour Party or stay alone from both has divided, split and, on some occasions, almost destroyed the party in Wales. It has also given us a wide array of politicians who have become heroes and villains of Welsh Liberal history.

SPLITS AND DIVISIONS

The first major split within the Liberal Party occurred in 1886 when Chamberlain, the arch Nonconformist, who had a great following in Wales, fell out with Prime Minister William Gladstone over Irish Home Rule. 'Home Rule' is what we now refer to as 'devolution' or in essence allowing Ireland to have its own parliament to make laws on its domestic affairs. Gladstone was very much for Home Rule, and Chamberlain very much against it. This caused a Liberal split, one of the biggest splits within a ruling party in British political history. Chamberlain's Liberals where now known as the Liberal Unionists. From this followed a trend of every different split creating a new brand of Liberals. In Wales, however, in the general election of that year there was only one Liberal Unionist success. This was Sir William Cornwallis-West in Wrexham. This victory was only because the Liberals failed to contest the seat and Cornwallis-West won unopposed. The Liberals won 26 of the remaining 33 constituencies in Wales. Chamberlain went into coalition with the Tories and in doing so became the first Liberal villain of coalition government.

Whilst there were some divisions within the Welsh Liberal party over the disestablishment of the Anglican Church in Wales, the Boer War and battles between the Welsh Liberal Nationalists and the Welsh Liberal traditionalists, there was no long lasting damage to the party in Wales during the Edwardian period. The Welsh Liberals at the start of the twentieth century were in opposition to a Conservative government that had won power on the back of the jingoism surrounding the Boer War but then soon found themselves struggling to retain power. Indeed by 1902, the Welsh Liberals, dubbed by the Conservative Press at the time as 'the Radicals', were almost wholly united in their rejection of the Conservative Arthur Balfour's 1902 Education Act.

This sought to make those voluntary schools run by the Anglican and Catholic churches funded by the local rate in future. To the largely secular or Nonconformist Welsh Liberals, this smacked of religious imperialism by the Conservative government. David Lloyd George led a successful rebellion of the Liberal-run Welsh councils, whose refusal to implement Balfour's hated Education Act made Lloyd George a Liberal hero.

Before the now widely despised Conservative government finally collapsed in late 1905, there was a period of Liberal and Conservative defections over the introduction of tariffs on trade. The Liberals as a party were against them and the Conservatives for them. In 1904, Cardiff's sitting Liberal MP, Sir Edward Reed, crossed the floor to join the Conservatives in support of trade tariffs. The Cardiff Liberals replaced Reed with the aristocrat, Ivor Churchill Guest.

Ivor Churchill Guest, Conservative and Liberal

He was a former Conservative MP, a Cardiff steel industrialist and cousin of Winston Churchill. Like his cousin, Ivor had also left the Conservatives over the issue of free trade. He earned his Liberal credentials and displayed his Liberal loyalty significantly enough to win the Cardiff seat at the 1906 Liberal landslide election. Ivor's brother, Christian, became the MP for Pembroke and Haverfordwest between 1910–1918 and his son was the National Liberal MP for Brecon and Radnor between 1935 and 1939. In the 1930s all of the Guests were to support the Conservatives either directly or as National Liberals casting them as villains to the wider Welsh Liberal Party.

WELSH LIBERAL NAME CHANGES AND COALITIONS 1916 TO PRESENT

Period party changed its name	Party split	Name change	Coalition	Where Welsh Liberal MPs stood
1916–1923	Yes	Coalition Liberals (Lloyd George Liberals)	Liberal-Conservative	Mainly backing Lloyd George
1916–1923	Yes	Liberals (Asquithian i.e. not in the coalition)	Liberal-Conservative	Only a few backed Asquith
1931–1948	Yes	Liberal Nationals	National Governments until 1945	A third of Welsh Liberal MPs
1931–1966	Yes	Liberals	National Governments until 1945	A third of Welsh Liberal MPs, moving to all Welsh Liberal MPs after 1950
1931–1935	Yes	Independent Liberals – Lloyd George Family Group	National Governments until 1945	The four Lloyd George family members
1966–1988	No	Welsh Liberal Party	Lib-Lab pact, 1977–78, 1981–1988 with SDP Alliance	All MPs kept the party name
1989	No	Welsh Social and Liberal Democratic Party	Merger with SDP	MPs reject notion of removing 'Liberal'
1989	No	Welsh Liberal Democrats	None until 2000	Supported by Welsh MPs
2000–2003	No	Welsh Liberal Democrats	Welsh Assembly Coalition government with Labour	No name change
2010–present	No	Welsh Liberal Democrats	Westminster Coalition government with Conservatives	No name change

David Lloyd George

After the Liberal landslide of 1906, it was just ten years before the Liberal Party in Wales, and across the wider UK, was split into two camps by the 'palace coup' in which Welsh Liberal MP David Lloyd George, supported by many Welsh Liberal MPs but also now for the first time by Conservative ones, displaced Herbert Asquith as Prime Minister. The Liberal Party now split between those who supported Lloyd George and those who carried on supporting Asquith's leadership of the party. In Wales there was close to civil war in some constituencies within the Liberal Party over whether or not to support the coalition. The 1921 by-election in Carmarthen, where coalition Liberal, with Conservative support, fought Asquithian Liberal was the most overt example of this.

The coalition government led by Lloyd George gave the Welsh Liberal Party its first ever prime minister but in the process saw it relegated to a slow lingering death that would never see the party's Welsh MPs play centre stage in government again. The coalition eventually collapsed when the Conservative backbenchers feared losing their own identity in a hybrid Lloyd George-led party. Coalition Liberals tactically fought the 1922 General Election with one hand behind their back, unable to attack their former Conservative coalition partners to any effective degree because they had been supporting the same policies, and not able to draw strength from the independence that the Asquithian Liberals could.

Lloyd George had held the loyalty of most Welsh Liberals during the seven years' split. Nevertheless not all Welsh Liberals endorsed his closeness to the Conservatives, their traditional foe. For Welsh Liberal MPs such as Sir Rhys Hopkin Morris (Cardigan) and David Davies (Montgomeryshire) Lloyd George had by now become a Liberal villain who was destroying their party. In 1926 the previously loyal and senior Welsh Liberal MP, Sir Alfred Mond (Carmarthen), also became so opposed to Lloyd George's proposals for the virtual nationalisation of agricultural land (the so-called Green Book policies) that he crossed the floor to the Conservatives. In the process Mond, later Lord Melchett, became a Welsh Liberal villain.

The 1930s saw the Liberals split into a series of different groups. Those MPs who joined the Liberal Nationals (who supported the National Government) also frequently became villains of their own Liberal Associations. The three North Wales Liberal MPs that joined the Liberal Nationals were all publicly condemned by their Liberal Associations and sent to political Coventry. Some like Clement Davies would in time rejoin the Liberals but others such as Sir Henry Morris Jones (Denbigh) were lost to the Liberals forever.

In July 1945, with David Lloyd George now dead, the Welsh Liberals had just seven MPs elected in Wales. One of these, David's son Gwilym, continued to work closely with the Conservatives and subsequently joined them ending up as Conservative Home Secretary a decade later. The remaining six Welsh Liberals now made up half of the UK Liberal Party and it was one of their MPs, Clement Davies, who became the leader of the UK Liberal Party. Between 1947 and 1950 the Conservatives offered Davies a number of opportunities to merge his party with them in a permanent coalition. Davies rejected them all and in the process made himself a national Liberal hero for keeping the Liberal party independent and alive.

LIB-LAB PACT

The Welsh Liberals became a state party in their own right in 1966, under the leadership of Emlyn Hooson. This gave them a great deal of independence from the party in London, including the ability to create their own policies, choose their own leaders and make their own rules on candidate selection. Despite this independence the Welsh Liberals' fortunes didn't improve much at election times and the next time they were close to government was during the period of the Lib-Lab pact from 1977–78. The most successful Welsh Liberal during this period was Geraint Howells, the Cardiganshire MP. He was able to get the Labour government in April 1978 to recognize the Farmer Union of Wales (FUW) as an official negotiating partner with the Ministry of Agriculture, Fisheries and Foods and the Welsh Office. This put them on an equal basis with the National Farmers Union. It was a very popular move amongst Welsh farmers and would remain one of Howells's proudest achievements. For Emlyn Hooson, however, the Lib-Lab pact made him a villain amongst the voters in his Montgomeryshire constituency for his support of the 'Yes' vote in the 1979 St David's Day devolution referendum. He subsequently lost his seat in that year's general election ending almost one hundred years of Liberal domination of the Montgomeryshire seat. He remained, however, a Liberal hero amongst the Welsh party's faithful for having kept the party going.

SDP – LIBERAL ALLIANCE YEARS

The arrival of the SDP in Wales gave a vital shot of electoral blood to the Welsh Liberals. Their number of councillors consequently doubled in the 1980s. At the same time they outpaced Labour in many Welsh seats and it looked for a time as if the long awaited post-war Liberal revival would occur in Wales with the SDP's help. When the parties merged in 1988 to become the Welsh Social and Liberal Democratic Party, the new party's fortune plummeted in both the opinion polls and at the ballot box. This caused party members to look once again at the overly long name. Various options arose including removing the name Liberal altogether. Welsh leader Howells, however, insisted that the new party was called 'Liberal Democrats' and not 'Social Democrats'. He used his position as Welsh Liberal party leader to apply this move to the wider UK. At the same time MPs Alex Carlile and Richard Livsey declared with Howells that from now on they would be known in Wales as the Welsh Liberal Democrats. They held a press conference in the House of Commons to announce their adopted name, which was duly reported in the Welsh press the next day and with that the name became fixed. Thus Howells had once again become a hero of the Welsh Liberals for saving their cherished name.

Geraint Howells (with bowler hat in hand) shares a joke with the Queen at the Royal Welsh Show

WELSH ASSEMBLY COALITION

The fall of First Secretary Alun Michael during the first term of the Welsh Assembly in 2000 led the way for a Labour-Liberal coalition between 2000 and 2003. The coalition had no impact on the Welsh Liberal Democrats' electoral fortunes as they remained stuck on six Assembly seats post-2003. It neither pushed them up as the party hoped or knocked them down as they feared. Although the problems associated with the party's Welsh leader Michael German's expenses in his former WJEC post proved damaging for him in the short term, this didn't hold either him or his deputy Jenny Randerson back in the long term. They both ended up going to the House of Lords. There would be no further coalition for the Welsh Liberal Democrats when they missed the political coalition boat post-2007 elections and ended up in opposition once more. In 2010, however, they entered the Westminster coalition with the Conservatives along with the rest of the Liberal Democrats.

ARE THE WELSH LIBERAL DEMOCRATS A DEFECTIVE PARTY?

Despite their history appearing to indicate the contrary, the Welsh Liberals have been remarkably loyal to their party whilst holding elected office. Gwilym Lloyd George was the last sitting Welsh Liberal MP to lose the party whip for failing to support the party and in effect become a member of another party – the Conservatives. That was in 1946. Since then no sitting Welsh Liberal

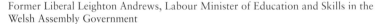

Former Liberal Leighton Andrews, Labour Minister of Education and Skills in the Welsh Assembly Government

Lord, Assembly Member or MP has defected to another political party. In addition remarkably few prospective or senior Liberal politicians have defected to other political parties. When they have occurred, defections to the Conservatives have been the most common. In the last fifty years only two of these defectors, Rene Kinzett in Swansea West and Felix Aubel (former SDP) in Brecon and Radnor, have come close to winning a parliamentary seat.

Three high profile defectors to the Labour Party did gain elected office in Wales. Two of these, Peter Hain and Leighton Andrews, however, had never stood for office in Wales as Liberals prior to standing for the Labour Party, so they were not really Welsh Liberal defectors. Megan Lloyd George, however, had been a very senior Welsh Liberal and long-serving MP for Anglesey. Megan joined the Labour Party in 1955. She had been close to Labour Party MPs including Clement Attlee for some years. Her defection was still a huge blow to the post-war Welsh Liberals particularly when she was elected at the 1957 Carmarthen by-election to replace the late Liberal MP Sir Rhys Hopkin Morris. In the process Megan, for such a long time a heroine of Welsh Liberalism, became a villain.

HAVE COALITIONS BENEFITED OR DESTROYED THE WELSH LIBERALS?

The main benefit of coalition prior to the 1960s was the fact that the Conservatives often let the Welsh Liberals have a free run at the seat against Labour. This aside, the Welsh electorate have either sought to punish the Welsh Liberals as allies of the main government, as they did in 1979 after the Lib-Lab pact and the 2011 Welsh Assembly Elections or shown indifference, as happened after the 2000–2003 Welsh Assembly Lib-Lab pact.

In the election of 1910 the Welsh Liberals had fought the election using the slogan 'The Liberals always deliver more than the Tories promise'. What they discovered, however, was that a few years later when they were in coalition with those same Tories, campaigning against them became a lot more complex because they had been allies. This same century-old problem is likely to occur in elections over the next four years.

Further reading:
Russell Deacon, *The Welsh Liberals: The History of the Liberal and Liberal Democrat parties in Wales* (2012)

22

ORDER! ORDER?
THE LIVES OF GEORGE THOMAS, VISCOUNT TONYPANDY

Paul O'Leary

Few politicians have won as much popular acclaim and affection as the Labour MP George Thomas, who became Speaker of the House of Commons and was later ennobled as Lord Tonypandy. When parliamentary proceedings were broadcast on radio for the first time in 1978 his voice – sonorously declaiming 'Order! Order!' – was used as the daily introduction to the BBC's *Today in Parliament* programme. Parliament now had a voice that could be heard in every household in the land, and that voice had an unmistakable Rhondda accent.

George Thomas admiring himself

Towards the end of his life he was something of a celebrity figure, spending his time on children's charity work and socialising with royalty and the great and the good. This view was summed up by his friend Margaret Thatcher, who described him as 'a deeply committed Christian with a shining integrity'.

During his long and varied public life there were many surprises that help us to see George Thomas as a more complicated figure than the later image he created would suggest. In some ways, he was a classic example of the 'Marmite politician' – deeply loved by many and equally deeply disliked by others. Moreover, parts of his life were more controversial and more complicated than the official version of his life suggested.

A very mottled character

Professor Glanmor Williams's description of George Thomas.

AN OFFICIAL LIFE

The view of Thomas as a public figure of 'shining integrity' became established at the height of his fame in the 1980s. It was a powerful image of the sincere and genuine public servant. This version of his life was circulated through his autobiography, which was published in 1985, and through several official or semi-official biographies that were published at that time. These books portray the life of a poor boy who endured genuine hardship when young, born in Port Talbot in 1909 and raised in the appalling circumstances of a difficult family life in the Rhondda valleys between the wars. The death of his father left the family in dire straits, but Thomas overcame these difficulties with the support of his remaining family. Education and politics were the main avenues that led to his future success in life. He went to grammar school and then to University College Southampton, before becoming a school teacher in Cardiff. He was an active member of the National Union of Teachers (NUT) and of the Labour Party, and he was elected MP for the constituency of Cardiff Central in the Labour landslide of 1945. From 1950 he was MP for Cardiff West. This was the beginning of a public career that led to a position in the Cabinet and a place in the House of Lords.

Throughout this journey he was sustained by his Methodism. By the end of his life he was a popular lay preacher on both sides of the Atlantic and on several occasions he lectured on the Christian heritage in politics. For much of his adult life he was supported by his mother. Emma Jane Thomas, or simply 'Mam,' as she was known to all, had been a Labour activist in her own right and accompanied her son on official business when he was a cabinet minister.

The fact that Thomas never lost his accent, despite being away from the Rhondda all his adult life, was widely seen as evidence of his continuing connection to his roots and a sign of his basic sincerity. Here was a prominent public figure who had stayed true to his origins. When he was awarded a viscountcy in 1983, he chose a name from the Rhondda valley that resonated in the annals of labour history – Tonypandy, site of the infamous riots of 1910. A man who considered himself a friend of royalty retained strong links with his people. Or so it seemed.

THE 'OUTLANDISH LEFT-WINGER'

According to his friend and Labour leader Harold Wilson, George Thomas was considered by some to be 'a somewhat outlandish left-winger'. When Wilson made this comment, it's likely that he had in mind a specific incident that happened in 1948. In that year, when he was still in his first term as an MP, Thomas visited Greece during the bitter civil war that was then dividing

Harold Wilson, with a rosetted James Callaghan

the country to act as observer at a controversial trial of Greek students accused of supporting the Republican rebels under General Markos. He made the trip on behalf of the National Union of Students.

In circumstances that remain rather mysterious, Thomas ended up making contact with Markos's forces in the mountains of Thessaly, and the British press was alive with speculation about his fate. When he finally returned from this strange episode, he conveyed a message from the rebels to the United Nations commission on Greek border troubles that was to be set up in Salonika, and he was extremely critical of his own government's policy of support for the Greek government. Subsequently, it appeared as though the MP from South Wales had been a pawn in the machinations of more powerful and secret forces. When he returned to Britain, Thomas complained to then Labour Prime Minister, Clement Attlee, that he had been set up by the British secret services and claimed that he was still under surveillance by MI5. Despite Attlee's initial scepticism about this claim, he agreed to enquire further and discovered that Thomas was, in fact, being watched by MI5. He ordered the surveillance to cease. Later, Thomas would put his actions down to naivety, but it probably consolidated his reputation as a maverick.

WHITE-COLLAR FIREBRAND

A reputation as a radical MP was consolidated during the 1950s, when Thomas was a spirited defender of the National Union of Teachers (NUT), the trade union that sponsored him. It's worth considering the experiences of Thomas and his fellow Cardiff Labour MP James Callaghan in this regard. Unlike the majority of South Wales Labour MPs, who were sponsored by the miners' union, both Callaghan and Thomas were supported by white-collar unions. But Callaghan's roots in the civil service unions made him instinctively more cautious, while Thomas gained a reputation as something of a firebrand.

In the 1950s, Thomas was on the left of the Labour Party and he campaigned against the hydrogen bomb, a stance that was consistent with the Christian pacifism he had espoused during the 1930s. He continued to be a campaigning MP into the 1960s. Probably the most important practical achievement of this period – possibly of his whole life – was championing leasehold reform. Thomas became identified with this campaign, though some of the campaigners dispute the centrality of his position in it. Whatever his precise role, the Leasehold Enfranchisement Bill (1967) solved a major problem relating to the housing stock in much of South Wales, where the effects of Victorian development were soon to be felt as many leases expired. The Bill enabled occupiers of leasehold property with a rateable value over £40 per annum to buy their property outright.

AT THE HEART OF GOVERNMENT

This achievement took place against a background of closer involvement in the business of government following Labour's successes in the general elections of 1964 and 1966. Thomas held government posts from 1964 to 1970, developing a career that embraced a number of Whitehall departments, moving steadily upwards from junior minister to minister of state and secretary of state. The personal trajectory of this radical backbencher was now at the heart of government.

His two explosive years as Secretary of State for Wales from 1968 to 1970 have come to define how many people in Wales react to him. Thomas had a barely disguised antipathy to his predecessor as Secretary of State for Wales, Cledwyn Hughes, who he saw as a traitor for trying to promote limited devolution. The defining events of Thomas's stint in Cathays Park were implacable opposition to nationalism, equally determined opposition to language pressure groups, a major miscalculation in deciding that part of the costs of removing the coal tip at Aberfan should be taken from the money donated to the families, and overseeing the Investiture of the Prince of Wales in 1969 at Caernarfon Castle. The Investiture was the beginning of Thomas's connections with monarchy

Cledwyn Hughes, Thomas's predecessor as Secretary of State for Wales

179

and the establishment. He came to see himself as an avuncular figure, shielding a young and inexperienced Prince Charles from the forces of nationalism.

These controversial events required a cool head and clever political footwork, but Thomas seemed to choose unerringly the intervention that would cause greatest upset. At a time of acute divisions in Welsh society Thomas's interventions fanned the flames of discord.

'ONE OF THE GREATEST ESTABLISHMENT CONVERTS OF HIS TIME'

Both Labour and nationalist commentators have claimed that Thomas was out of touch with new social and cultural developments of the period. It is difficult to disagree with this judgement. For his part, Thomas seemed not to realise this and expected to resume his position at the Welsh Office when Labour returned to government in 1974, but he was to be disappointed. According to Barbara Castle, Harold Wilson was determined to move him out of the cabinet. Thus it was that in 1974 Thomas became Deputy Speaker and Chairman of Ways and Means. There was no guarantee that he would become Speaker when the post became vacant in 1976, as that appointment was in the gift of the House of Commons, not the government. This move sideways in political terms was accompanied by his increasing distance from the Labour Party.

This was partly a consequence of not contesting elections, as is the custom with the Speaker, so that he seemed to rise above the partisan fray. But his estrangement from the party went beyond this. There are opposing views about how this affected his performance as Speaker. James Callaghan claimed that Thomas made decisions as Speaker that made life unnecessarily difficult for the Labour government, while the views of other politicians were more mixed.

It was becoming clear that Thomas's political sympathies had shifted to the right. He developed a close friendship with Margaret Thatcher, to the extent that he visited the Thatchers for Christmas lunch at Chequers while he was still Speaker of the Commons. At best, this was unwise. He also exchanged presents with Thatcher, whereas there was no comparable relationship with the Labour leader of the Opposition.

By the early 1980s he had come to see Thatcher as the only person who could save Britain from its social and economic difficulties. Favouring one party leader over another in this explicit way was a dangerous course of action for a Speaker to take, especially as the person in question was the Prime

Minister. The gulf between Thomas and the Labour Party became even clearer when he retired from the Commons in 1983 and joined the House of Lords.

One sign of changing attitudes was the publication of his memoirs in 1985. Thomas used the book to settle scores with people who had previously been political friends and allies, like James Callaghan and Michael Foot. Thomas had been jealous of Callaghan since the latter, wearing his naval uniform, had beaten him to the nomination for one of the Cardiff seats in 1945. By contrast,

Michael Foot, a previous political friend and ally of George Thomas

the friends he now cultivated were those who had money, prestige and rank, like the banker and tax exile Julian Hodge. This friendship led to Thomas becoming chairman of the Bank of Wales between 1983 and 1991. He was also close to the Saudi oil minister Sheikh Yamani at this time.

One of the political touchstones of these years was attitudes to the European Union, the issue on which the Conservative Party nearly broke itself in the 1990s. On this issue George Thomas sided with the right-wingers. In fact, he went further than many Conservatives by supporting the maverick millionaire financier Sir James Goldsmith and his Referendum Party. Following his period of fame as Speaker of the Commons, Viscount Tonypandy was paraded as the great defender of parliamentary traditions. His personal endorsement of this fringe party, delivered against the backdrop of a waving Union flag, was used as the rousing culmination of a Referendum Party video.

By this date, then, Thomas had moved right across the political spectrum, from the left wing of the Labour Party to support for an organisation funded by a millionaire to the right of the Tory Party. This party espoused an aggressive form of British nationalism. It is more than a little ironic that the implacable opponent of Welsh nationalism in the 1960s now adopted the stance of flag-waver-in-chief to the British right.

This change in political sympathies went hand in hand with a rather different social life to that of the average South Wales Labour MP. One indication of this was an increasing penchant for socialising with the English upper classes and members of the Tory party.

One of the greatest establishment converts of his time

Conservative MP Robert Rhodes James of George Thomas

Whereas previously he had seemed like someone who had stayed true to his origins, it was possible now to see quite how far he had travelled from his roots.

'SECRET HOMOSEXUAL, SUPERB SPEAKER OF THE HOUSE OF COMMONS'

George Thomas's life seemed to have come full circle. Following his death in 1997, however, there were revelations about his personal life that challenged what many people thought they knew about the man and the politician.

Leo Abse – a close personal friend for many years – wrote about Thomas's life with the following striking sentence: 'George Thomas, secret homosexual, superb Speaker of the House of Commons, was no saint; nor did he claim to be one.' Abse documented a number of cases when Thomas had been threatened with blackmail because of his sexuality. He claimed that the need to conceal his sexuality throughout his life because of punitive legislation and intolerant social attitudes meant that he was engaged in a continual battle with his own 'unworthiness'. Instead of underlining the many achievements of Thomas's successful public career, Abse spoke of 'the thin ice upon which he skated all his life'.

If we are to believe Leo Abse, the brash confident school teacher and inspirational lay preacher was much more uncertain of himself than the carefully crafted public image would suggest. According to this view, the man behind the broad smile was tortured by the compromises he had to make because of his private life.

How does this affect the way we think of George Thomas? Probably his supporters and critics will still see him as either a hero or a villain, according to their political standpoints. However, we can go beyond this polarised division and begin to see the man and the politician as an historical figure who grappled with difficulties as well as enjoying the privileges of success. Taking on board the fact of his sexuality allows us to revise what we think we know and ask new questions.

Further reading:
Paul O'Leary, 'The Problems of Political Biography: the Lives of George Thomas, Viscount Tonypandy (1909–1997)', *Transactions of the Honourable Society of Cymmrodorion 2007*, Vol. 14 (2008), pp. 162–74

23

THE HEROES OF RECENT WELSH POLITICAL HISTORY

Martin Johnes

Politics is not what it once was. The 'No' campaign in the 2011 Referendum made much of its (misleading) claim that a 'Yes' vote would lead to the creation of more politicians. The cynicism about party politics is only too evident in falling turnouts at elections. It culminated in the anger that greeted the 2009 parliamentary expenses scandal.

Politicians may now be reviled in terms once reserved for estate agents but there have been a number since the Second World War who have transcended such mistrusts and can be regarded as heroes.

GWYNFOR

Shortly after the 1966 General Election, Megan Lloyd George, the Labour MP for Carmarthen, died. This meant a by-election at a time when the Labour government was being criticised for its financial policies and struggling to cope with internal strife. Within the constituency itself, there were significant concerns that local collieries and rural schools might close; farmers were worrying about small-business taxes. The scene was set for one of the biggest shocks of modern political history.

Gwynfor Evans on the campaign trail

Plaid Cymru's candidate was its president Gwynfor Evans. The party had finished third in the recent general election, with nearly 14,000 fewer votes than Labour, and bookmakers were apparently offering odds of 2,000 to 1 on Evans taking the seat. But take the seat he did, and with a majority of 2,436. Outside the count, a crowd of 2,000 sang the national anthem and waved Welsh flags. The local newspaper called it the 'Election of the Century'.

Although Evans had been the party's president since 1945, his political career had been one of disappointment and failures. But now, suddenly and unexpectedly, he was a hero, and not just for Welsh nationalists. He impressed the right-wing press in England. They took to him not as a Welsh nationalist but as someone who represented the concerns of ordinary people against an aloof, bloated and unpopular government.

When Evans took his seat in Parliament, the *Daily Mirror* described it as 'one of those highly-emotional occasions the Welsh do so well. All leeks and flags, hymns and chants'. Supporters sang the national anthem five times outside Parliament and gave Evans a reception of the 'fervour and enthusiasm they usually reserve for a winning try at Cardiff Arms Park (against England, of course)'.

The voters of Carmarthen salute Gwynfor Evans's 1966 General Election victory

Such moments are passing but Evans's reputation as the most important Welsh nationalist and one of the most important Welsh politicians of all time was secured by his threats to starve himself to death unless Mrs Thatcher's government honoured its manifesto commitment to create a Welsh-language television channel. Government archives show the threat was taken very seriously and was central to the government giving in. Even those who were not nationalists could appreciate the sight of the Conservatives backing down to Welsh pressure.

There's been nothing like it since the Beatles were here

A remark by a porter at the House of Commons on the day that Gwynfor Evans took his seat

The incident illustrates how selective popular memory can be. Before the S4C saga, the hope of 1966 had faded and there was actually a widespread belief that Evans had failed to deliver on Plaid's potential. Indeed, his determination to stand firm on this issue may have been to make up for his past failures. Gwynfor won and his heroic place in Welsh history was secured. It only takes one victory to outshine all the failures.

NYE

Yet one man's hero is another man's villain. Amongst segments of the Labour party, Evans was reviled. Afraid of what he stood for and its potential impact on their own base of support, some Labour MPs refused to speak to Evans or even look at him when he was first elected to the Commons. Their hero was Aneurin Bevan. They saw him as someone driven by the common good rather than the cause of one nation or one class. His elevation above other Labour figures rested on his baiting of selfish Tories and his central role in the creation of the National Health Service.

The NHS remains probably the greatest achievement in modern British political history. It is also a service used by nearly everyone in the UK at some point in their lives. For the poor in particular, it could be the difference between life and death. It is thus something worthy of celebration and it turned its maker into a symbol of a Welsh commitment to communities and social justice.

In 1987 Labour-controlled South Glamorgan County Council put up a statue of Bevan in the heart of Cardiff's shopping district. Bevan had no real link with Cardiff and his image was being employed as a statement of the authority's ideals and political sympathies at a time when local government was under repeated attack from a Conservative government. So powerful was Bevan's symbolic status that in subsequent years, streets, a pub and a health trust have all been named after him.

The reverence, however, was not universal, and his Cardiff statue is regularly adorned with a traffic cone by revellers uninterested in celebrating him. The reality of his life was also more complex than his symbolism suggests. When he died in 1960, he was relatively wealthy and living on a large farm in Buckinghamshire. He enjoyed the good life and had come a long way from his roots, no matter how much he still symbolized them.

Nor was his political career wholly successful. As a minister in the post-war Labour government, he had also been responsible for housing. This was an arena where the government failed to meet people's expectations and the disappointment was central to the party losing power in 1951. Bevan also never rose to the Labour leadership, and his political manoeuvrings helped divide the party and soured his personal relationships with colleagues. Also now largely forgotten is his later commitment to nuclear weapons. This hardly fits in with the idealistic picture of a state that prioritises putting resources into improving the lives of ordinary people.

None of this should undermine the idea of Nye as a hero but it is a reminder of how selective history can be.

TORIES TOO

There are also other figures in recent Welsh political history who have achieved much, but in quieter, less obvious ways. One such person is Sir Wyn Roberts.

A Welsh-speaking North Walian, Roberts held a ministerial post from 1979 to 1994. He had deep traditional Welsh sympathies and ensured that the language had someone with its best interests at heart at the centre of the Welsh Office. A special adviser in the department noted that whenever John Major was asked about Welsh issues he always asked 'Does Wyn think it's important?' Roberts played a central role in the 1993 Welsh Language Act. This piece of legislation was much criticised for what it did not do but it was central to giving bilingualism a symbolic but compulsory place in public life, on public signs and on public forms. In doing so it provided a very visible symbol to people in and outside Wales that this was not England.

That mattered in keeping alive and relevant a sense of Welsh nationality and it was also building on the establishment of a Welsh national curriculum. Again, Roberts was central to making this happen. It ensured that every Welsh schoolchild had at least a smattering of knowledge of the Welsh language and Welsh history. After decades where the very survival of Wales as a distinct nation had been a source of concern, these things mattered, at least to those who value the existence of a Welsh nation.

Roberts's reputation was tarnished by the fact he was a Conservative. Although the Tory governments of 1979 to 1997 were never as unpopular as accepted memory suggests, they do not have a positive reputation in Wales. Roberts never became a hero, not because of his own failings but because of the wider actions of the government he was a member of.

The history of Margaret Thatcher's government also illustrates the importance of looking beyond Wales's borders for its political heroes and villains. Thatcher's economic record meant she was genuinely unpopular, not least in coalmining communities where she developed a reputation more akin to an antichrist than a villain. Of course, the fact that she was English did not help her case and it added to the sense that she did not understand the Welsh working-class communities which people felt she was destroying.

But being English did not have to be a barrier to being a political hero in Wales. This is clear when the career of Winston Churchill is considered. The man who led Britain to victory in the Second World War was certainly not universally popular in Wales. Before the war he had been something of a hate figure amongst the South Wales miners because of his decision to send troops to the Rhondda following the Tonypandy riots of 1910. Although they never fired on crowds, the fact that they were deployed at all was taken as a great insult and a huge overreaction.

But the Second World War saw memories fade and the Churchill of angry stories was replaced by the one on the radio inspiring people to stand firm and fight for victory. Not everyone was impressed but the crisis of war meant older rivalries were put aside. When Churchill died in 1965 there was an outpouring of grief and respect across Wales. Even in the Rhondda, the local paper reported 'a general air of sadness as our people join in the worldwide mourning for the death of the greatest statesman of our time'. There were tributes paid in local churches, chapels and pubs. Some shops even put draped photographs of him in the window.

Winston Churchill, Welsh political hero?

Rhodri Morgan, former First Minister

RHODRI

Churchill's heroic status was recognized by contemporaries but others have to wait for historians to accord them the credit they deserve. One such figure is Rhodri Morgan.

Beyond Ron Davies, better known for his scandals than his very real contribution to the establishment of devolution, Morgan remains the only figure in the history of Welsh devolution with any real public profile. The media was often keen to stress his 'man of the people' credentials but the wider Welsh public was less interested in the politician who led the Assembly for nearly a decade. At the 2007 National Assembly election, turnout in Morgan's ward was 42% and he received 39% of the votes that were cast. Thus only 16% of his constituency voted for Morgan. Many people do not know who he is. Only 43% of people in a 2007 poll for the BBC could name him.

Yet Welsh history will accord Morgan a very prominent place. His achievement was not anything devolved politics did under him but the way it became accepted as a legitimate means of governing Wales. Just one in four of the Welsh electorate had voted for devolution in 1997 but, by the time of Morgan's resignation as First Minister in 2009, opinion polls suggested that just 15% of people wanted to see the Assembly abolished. It might not have changed much about life in Wales or won widespread affection, but people accepted devolution and that owed much to Morgan's careful leadership. After a choppy beginning under Alun Michael, Morgan steered the Assembly into calmer waters when it might easily have sunk.

ACTIVISTS

Morgan won little popular credit for his achievements because by the end of the twentieth century the public's faith in mainstream politics had faded. This was a long-term and gradual process that had been gaining pace since the 1960s. By the age of devolution, a majority of people were choosing to not even vote in Welsh elections, let alone turn any of their representatives into heroes. That did not mean people were not interested in political issues. This was clear in how from the 1960s a new type of political hero was emerging, the activist.

In Wales one such figure was Dafydd Iwan. He was an architect by profession but was best known as a folk singer and for his role in putting the Welsh language on the political map. Iwan was chair of the Welsh Language Society from 1968 to 1971, a period when its campaigning was at its height. The vandalising of road signs in particular won the language cause publicity across the UK and was instrumental in the gradual shift to bilingual signage and provision across public life in Wales.

Dafydd Iwan, folk singer, activist and politician

Both the causes and the tactics of the Welsh Language Society enraged as much as they inspired. Iwan may have been a hero to some but to others he was a long-haired, irresponsible vandal. Even those who sympathized with the cause could be offended by the methods. Iwan may have nominally led this campaign but it was a movement of some 2,000 people. By 1976, 697 individuals had appeared in court and 143 had been imprisoned for their part in the society's actions.

It is thus rather misleading to identify one individual as being its hero. Many of the greatest political heroes are anonymous figures who neither sought nor gained personal recognition for what they did. A movement or trade union might have figureheads but it is the willingness of individuals to strike, protest and make sacrifices for a cause that so often forces political change.

MAKING A DIFFERENCE

The language protestors in Wales clearly saw themselves as part of a wider global movement and they were inspired by Martin Luther King and its other figureheads. They were evidence of how far the influence of political heroes can spread. A biography of King was one of the bestselling Welsh-language books of 1969. It claimed that, having being held down for centuries himself, a Welshman could understand the oppression of black Americans.

It was an entirely misleading comparison. Never in the modern period were Wales and the Welsh overtly oppressed in anything that resembled slavery or the abuse of dignity and rights that still followed its abolition. Welsh injustices may not have been as terrible as those in many parts of the world but this does not devalue those who have laboured to make Wales a better place, whether that meant enhancing the position of a particular culture or class.

Not everyone might agree on what the problems or the solutions are, but the recent political history of Wales does show that individuals, be they famous politicians or anonymous citizens, can make a difference. In a cynical and fatalistic age that is something worth thinking about.

Further reading:
Martin Johnes, *Wales since 1939* (2012)

190

24

THE WELSH RUGBY TEAM: THE ULTIMATE WELSH HEROES?

Martin Johnes

On February 19, 1881, a team of Welsh ex-public schoolboys visited London to play Wales's first ever rugby international. The match was not well organised and the Welsh team turned up two players short. Replacements were found from the crowd and it was thus perhaps not surprising that the result was a thumping. England scored six tries, while Wales failed to register a single point. On this occasion the Welsh rugby team were neither heroes nor villains. The truth was that no one much noticed or cared about the match. However, over the course of the following century, not only did people begin to care, often very deeply, about rugby but the game came to help define Wales itself.

A TEAM OF SUPERMEN

If there was a moment that kicked that process into play it was on a December afternoon in 1905. Before 47,000, New Zealand visited the Arms Park at the end of a successful tour that had seen the tourists defeat the other home nations. Wales won 3–0. They had beaten the world's greatest team and restored the honour of the British motherland.

Contemporary writers got rather carried away. They saw the match as a moment of glory, not only for a triumphant nation but a triumphant race too. The editorial of one newspaper declared that Wales's qualities of defence and attack were racial and had been developed by history when powerful enemies drove the Welsh to their mountain fortresses. This had developed in the Welsh 'sons of strong determination, invincible stamina, resolute, mentally keen, physically sound'. Such talk suggested this was not just a team of heroes but of supermen.

For all the rhetoric of Celtic racial superiority, three members of the team were actually born in England. The press may have ignored this but the make-up of the national side actually helped rugby establish itself as an icon of Welshness and the players as popular heroes. Between 1861 and 1911 more than 227,000 people moved from England to the South Wales coalfield in search of work. Thus the fact that the national rugby team contained immigrants made it more representative of Wales, not less.

MORE EXCITING THAN POLITICS

One such player was Gwyn Nicholls, who had moved to Wales with his family from the West Country as a child. As a successful businessman who ran a Cardiff laundry company, he was not a likely hero of the working classes. But a hero he was. Whatever the social gap between him and the majority of rugby fans, he was a brilliant runner, passer and tackler. Such back play contrasted with the forward-dominated spheres of English and Scottish rugby and it helped establish Wales as the leading rugby nation in the British Isles. The result was seven championships and six triple crowns between 1900 and 1911.

It was in this success, and the passing and running that helped deliver the victories, that the popularity of Welsh rugby players lay. Quite simply, they were entertaining to watch and they delivered the results that people craved. The public school ethos that it was the taking part that mattered may have been persuasive in England but Welsh working-class audiences wanted teams that won. In 1908, David Lloyd George, the most famous Welshman of the day, saw his first match. He exclaimed, 'I must say I think it's more exciting than politics'. Any doubt that the best players really were popular heroes was dispelled by the 1910 Tonypandy riots. An angry crowd of miners smashed and looted store windows but carefully avoided the chemist shop of Willie Llewellyn who had played on the right wing for Wales.

OUR HEROES

Men like Llewellyn lived and worked in the communities in which they played. In contrast to football, where from the earliest days of professionalism the best players tended to head to England, rugby stars remained in Wales. They might be lured, sometimes by generous expenses and under-the-counter payments, to the bigger, more glamorous teams, but the majority stayed in Wales and this remained true until the advent of professionalism in 1995.

192

By staying in Wales, rugby stars forged close connections with their audiences. The players were a mixture of English and Welsh speakers and a combination of manual workers and the products of grammar schools. They were thus a reflection of the nation they represented. But their hero status was more than this. They were people you lived near, saw on the bus and on the street, and maybe even worked with. You could buy them a pint, listen to their stories and talk rugby with them. This gave people a sense of ownership of their rugby heroes that was different to the adulation aimed at movie or musical stars. With them, remoteness and unattainability was part of the appeal, but in rugby it was quite the opposite.

THE HERO WHO NEVER HAS TO BUY A DRINK

The hero status this accorded players could compensate for the missed financial rewards enforced by amateurism. Rugby opened doors for players in business, where their fame was attractive to both employer and customer. People wanted to be associated with the best players, which also meant that there were free meals, drinks and holidays to be enjoyed. John Taylor, who played for Wales between 1967 and 1973, thus said of his fellow internationals, 'He will undoubtedly have better job prospects than his peers and will also enjoy the benefits of being a celebrity. Anything from suits to motor cars will be offered at trade prices and if he can stand the non-stop questions on the game, he will never have to buy a drink.'

John Taylor

SMOTHERED BY KINDNESS

But being a hero in the communities in which you lived and worked was not always very pleasant. It certainly curtailed players' freedom. The constant requests to talk rugby and shake your hand could become suffocating. Clem Thomas, an international in the 1950s, called the rugby fraternity 'a brotherhood of friendship so embracing that at times it threatens to smother you and kill you with kindness'. J.P.R. Williams noted that international players were treated but also expected to behave like royalty. With Barry John, nicknamed the King, this even reached the level of a woman curtsying to him. John's experiences also signalled how the treatment of rugby's biggest stars was beginning to be affected by an emerging celebrity culture in sport.

Television was raising the profile of the game but, from the 1960s onwards, there also was more money about, less deference to individuals' privacy and more media interest in what stars did off the field. Shows like *A Question of Sport* broadcast players into the front rooms of the UK in their everyday attire, allowing them to become personalities rather than just players. They were even now in colour. Barry John thus found himself something propelled into a showbiz world where he mixed with the likes of George Best, the most famous sportsman in the land. But, like Best, John felt as if he was living in a 'goldfish bowl'. The constant attention became too much and he retired in 1972 to regain his freedom and privacy. He was 27.

The growing hero status accorded to rugby stars was partly about the renewed success on the pitch. Between 1969 and 1979, Wales won the Five Nations championship six times, collecting three grand slams and six triple crowns in the process. But players' status was also, as it had been in the first golden age before the First World War, based on the spectacular manner of the success and the nature of Welsh rugby culture itself.

Rugby was a game that people played as well as watched. Those who had played the game could appreciate the intricacies of a player's ability. They knew just how hard it was to make that run, sell that dummy or place that kick. For rugby aficionados, watching a game was not like being entertained by a musical masterpiece that they could never attempt themselves. It was watching someone do something that you had done yourself, just nowhere near as well.

But even those who were not interested in rugby could revere a local player who had won his cap. Such figures were not just representing their nation but their community too. In this sense their hero status drew not so much upon rugby but upon social aspiration and local pride. Like those who had done something with their lives in education or work, they were village or neighbourhood boys who had 'done well' and they were celebrated for it.

MAKING HEROES

What players achieved on the pitch was only witnessed first-hand by a minority. Before the televising of internationals in the 1950s, the vast majority of people could only read about games in the press or listen to them on the radio. This put fans at the mercy of journalists' interpretations of who had played well and whether there was cause to celebrate or commiserate.

Even after television, journalists and pundits remained very important in interpreting the game for people. Rugby is, after all, a very technical game and it is difficult to appreciate its finer points, especially when it comes to forward play. Some could make their own judgements based on their experience of playing, but even they were guided by the comments of commentators and writers.

People did not believe everything they read or heard, but the press box played a central role in deciding whether players were heroes or villains. It was no different for those in the stadium. After all, it is very difficult to see what is happening in a ruck or scrum from the far distance of the stands. This was a key reason why it was the backs that were often the biggest heroes. Quite simply, it was easier to see and understand what they were doing.

VILLAINS

Whether they understood rugby properly or not, fans often offered players their own critiques and suggestions. Everyone was an expert and knew best. But only in the 1970s were Welsh expectations so raised that defeats were seen as catastrophes and players were harangued by those who had never played the game at any decent level. By the end of the century, the development of the 'phone in' was even making these cutting criticisms public. A bad pass or a missed tackle, let alone a defeat, could suddenly turn heroes into villains.

It was not just when the team was performing badly that they might be thought of as villains. While supporters understood the financial temptations to switch 'codes' to rugby league, there was always a feeling that this also somehow represented letting Wales down. It was more understandable in the dark days of the inter-war depression, but in later years past heroes could be asked to leave their local clubhouses because they had subsequently 'gone north'. As the proverb went, there were three things best not discussed in polite Welsh society: politics, religion and rugby league.

It was only followers of rugby who could turn players into villains. In the 1970s the rugby widow was a staple theme of jokes and newspaper cartoons. Of course, the woman who was mistreated or forgotten by her rugby-mad man was a stereotype, but behind every stereotype runs a grain of truth. For these women there was little heroic about the players with whom they had to compete for their husband's attention and affection.

In North Wales too there could be much cursing of rugby. There football was far more popular and people were easily annoyed by how the Welsh and British media talked about a 'national' obsession. Rugby was another sign that Cardiff and the South were simply unaware of what North Wales was like.

More so than the players, it was often the selectors who were seen as the real villains. They were regularly accused of being ignorant or having favourites. Sometimes this was not unfair. In 1930, even the Lions chose Howard Poole, the Cardiff scrum-half who was yet to be capped by Wales. But at other times the reputation of selectors for not recognizing talent allowed old men to tell tales of how they could have played for Wales if only it hadn't been for a selector who preferred men from his own town.

PROFESSIONAL CELEBRITIES

In 1995 more than a century of rugby tradition was swept aside when the game went professional. Given the under-the-counter payments that had always happened, this was not quite the momentous shift that it first appeared but it was a real change nonetheless.

It opened the way for the regionalization of clubs and the emergence of rugby players that were not just paid but wealthy. This put a symbolic gap between the players and fans, and undermined the close bond between the two that helped make heroes. It was harder to think of players 'as one of us' when they earned more, drove bigger cars, lived in bigger houses and did not have normal jobs.

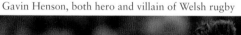

Gavin Henson, both hero and villain of Welsh rugby

The game's financial needs also saw it embrace advertising, thrusting its stars onto billboards and beer mats. Rugby was more visible than ever but its stars were more elusive and more remote. That was epitomised by Gavin Henson, with his slick hair and protruding muscles. Rugby players may always have been desirable to some women but the rugby star as sex symbol had now arrived. Females who had never taken any notice of rugby before were admiring him, not on the field of play but in the pages of celebrity magazines and on a television show about ballroom dancing.

Not all the team were even Welsh anymore after Graham Henry began selecting players whose links with Wales were remote and sometimes somewhat dubious. This culminated in the 2000 'Grannygate scandal', when the Welsh ancestry of two capped players turned out to be false.

James Hook, a thoroughly modern rugby professional and hero

PATRIOTS SO GOOD

In 2011, James Hook joined Perpignan for a salary reputedly worth more than a £1m over three years. There was surprise but no outrage. After all, this was still a modest sum by the standards of football's Premiership. For all the changes professionalization had brought, the financial and lifestyle gap between players and supporters was nothing like in football's highest echelons. Moreover, even if the nature of heroism in Welsh rugby had changed, players like Hook remained heroes with whom people could identify. There was still for many the understanding of how special stars' skills were because they had played the game themselves. There was also the common bond, most of the time at least, of being Welsh.

For all the razzmatazz and extortionate ticket prices of a contemporary international at the Millennium Stadium, there was one obvious link with match days gone-by and between supporters and players. All were proud of Wales. Fans could still see it on the players' faces as the camera closed in during the singing of the national anthem. A cynic might suggest that players know this will happen and that they consequently make sure they are both singing and looking like they feel it. A cynic might suggest that in doing so they are playing the modern celebrity game of acting up to the camera.

But if we were all cynics there would never be any heroes. Witnessing the joy on Shane Williams or James Hook's face when Wales win, it is hard for us not to believe that the players want it as much as we do. And that is why the Welsh rugby team remain heroes.

Further reading:
Martin Johnes, *A History of Sport in Wales* (2005)

Shane Williams scores the second of his two tries against Scotland in Cardiff, 2008

Notes on Contributors

Robin Barlow is Higher Education Advisor, Recruitment and Admissions, at Aberystwyth University

H.V. Bowen is Professor of Modern History at Swansea University and Convenor of History Research Wales

Lloyd Bowen is Senior Lecturer in Early Modern and Welsh History at Cardiff University

Ben Curtis is a Research Associate at Aberystwyth University and a History tutor at the Lifelong Learning Centre at Cardiff University

Russell Deacon is a part-time tutor at University of Wales – Trinity St David

Chris Evans is Professor of History at the University of Glamorgan

Madeleine Gray is Reader in History at University of Wales, Newport

Ray Howell is Professor of Welsh Antiquity at University of Wales, Newport

Martin Johnes is Senior Lecturer in History at Swansea University

Richard Marsden teaches History at Cardiff University and the Open University

Gethin Matthews is Lecturer in History at Swansea University, a post funded by the Coleg Cymraeg Cenedlaethol

Iwan Rhys Morus is Professor of History at Aberystwyth University

 Helen J. Nicholson is Reader in History at Cardiff University

 Katharine Olson is Lecturer in Medieval and Early Modern History at Bangor University

 Paul O'Leary is Senior Lecturer in Welsh History at Aberystwyth University

 Peter Stead is a writer and broadcaster, and Visiting Professor at the University of Glamorgan

 Toby Thacker is Lecturer in Modern European History at Cardiff University

 Noel Thompson is Professor of History at Swansea University

 Steven Thompson is Lecturer in Modern History at Aberystwyth University

 Chris Williams is Professor of Welsh History at Swansea University

 Sian Rhiannon Williams is Senior Lecturer in Education at Cardiff Metropolitan University

 Alun Withey is Lecturer in History at Swansea University

 David Wyatt is Lecturer in Early Medieval History, Community and Engagement at Cardiff University